WILLIAM A. FRASSANITO

GETTYSBURG

A JOURNEY IN TIME

CHARLES SCRIBNER'S SONS/NEW YORK

Charles Scribner's Sons
Macmillan Publishing Company
866 Third Avenue, New York, NY 10022
Collier Macmillan Canada, Inc.

Library of Congress Cataloging-in-Publication Data

Frassanito, William A.
  Gettysburg: a journey in time.

  Includes bibliographical references.
  1. Gettysburg, Battle of, 1863–Pictorial works.
2. Photography in historiography. I. Title.
E475.53.F793   973.7'349'0222   74-10597
ISBN 0-684-14696-7 (paper)

Macmillan books are available at special discounts for bulk purchases for sales promotions, premiums, fund-raising, or educational use. For details, contact:

    Special Sales Director
    Macmillan Publishing Company
    866 Third Avenue
    New York, NY 10022

            16   17   18   19   20

The picture on p. 114 is reprinted from *The Photographic History of the Civil War*, Francis T. Miller, ed. (New York: Review of Reviews Co., 1911) by permission of A. S. Barnes & Company, Inc.

Printed in the United States of America

GETTYSBURG

A JOURNEY IN TIME

To my parents, Americo and Edythe Frassanito

CONTENTS

ACKNOWLEDGMENTS

Many people have made significant contributions both during the research and the writing of this book. The author wishes to thank, first and foremost, Mr. William C. Darrah of Gettysburg, for the great interest he has shown in my work and the invaluable assistance he has given during many hours of discussion. The cooperation of Colonel Met Sheads and other staff members of the National Park Service at Gettysburg is likewise greatly appreciated, as is the assistance provided by the staff at the Library of Congress, the National Archives, the Gettysburg College library, the Adams County Historical Society, the New York Public Library, the New York Historical Society, and the New York State Historical Association.

Thanks are also due Miss Josephine Cobb of Washington, D.C.; Mr. Gordon Hoffman of Green Lake, Wisconsin; Mr. Frederick Rath of Cooperstown, New York; Mr. Donald Tyson of Gardners, Pennsylvania, for providing photographs and information regarding his ancestors; and Mrs. Sylvia Alexander of Glen Cove, New York, for typing the manuscript.

Additionally, I would like to extend a hearty thanks to my "hosts"—those friends who opened their doors to me during my extended research jaunts. They include Mr. and Mrs. Minor Wine Thomas of Cooperstown, New York, and the Eta Phi chapter of Alpha Chi Rho Fraternity at Gettysburg College. Four brothers of Alpha Chi Rho deserve mention for posing in the modern versions of views III-3, 6, and 14. They are Paul Hitchens, Todd Schonenberg, Bob Stephenson, and Andy Yurick.

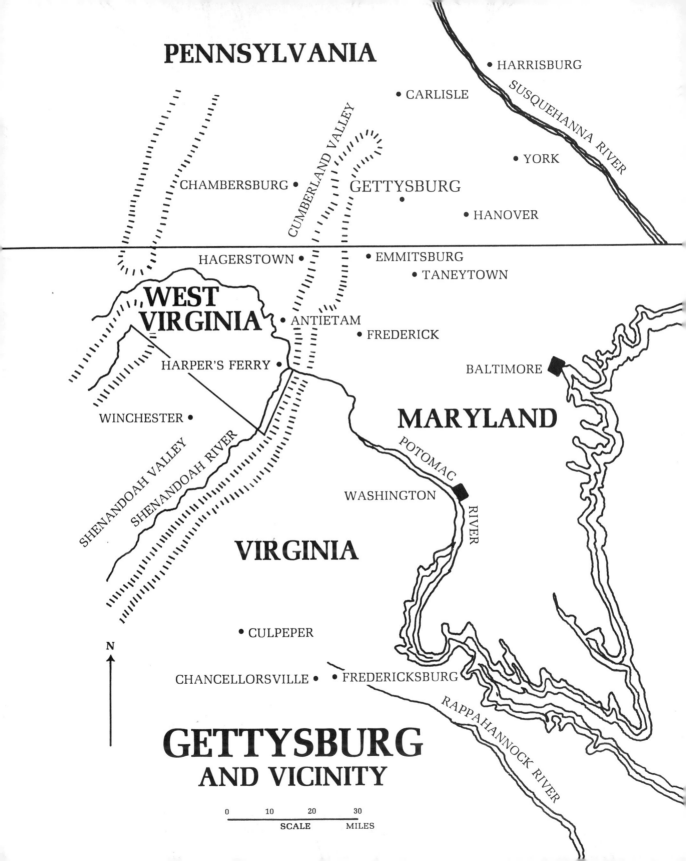

GETTYSBURG
AND VICINITY

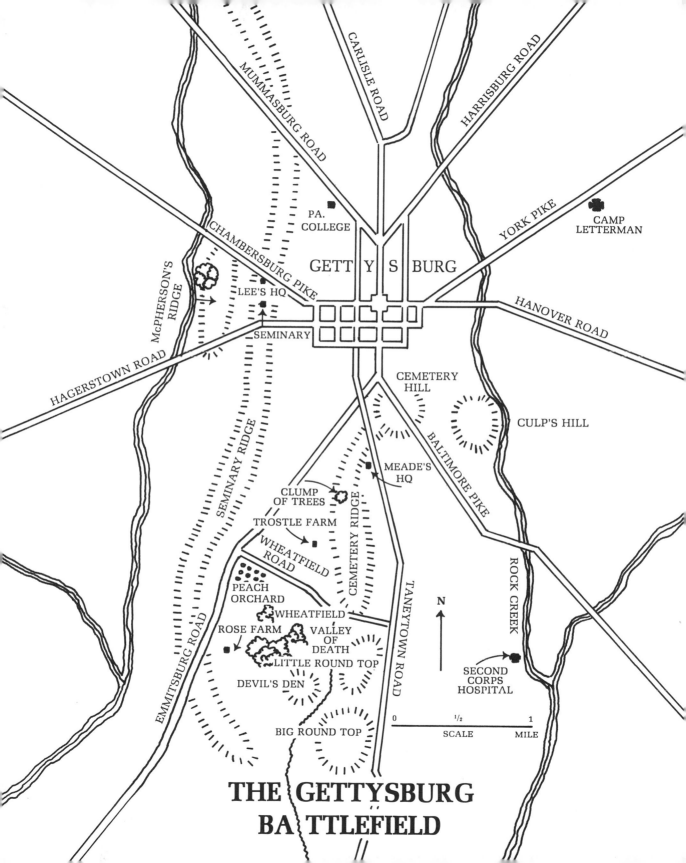

THE GETTYSBURG
BATTLEFIELD

PART ONE
THE PROBLEM

1

THE GETTYSBURG PHOTOGRAPHS
A NEW APPROACH

During the first three days of July 1863, one of the greatest battles in American history was fought on a twenty-five square mile tract of land surrounding the town of Gettysburg, Pennsylvania. Since that time, over one hundred years ago, literally thousands of books, pamphlets, and articles have been written to describe and analyze the battle, the field, the town and its immortal cemetery, the generals both Northern and Southern, and a host of related topics.

One aspect of this rich heritage, however, has never been given the attention it has so long deserved: the story of the photographers who came to Gettysburg both soon after the fighting and for several years thereafter to record for all time the battlefield's appearance during the mid-1860s. Never can their work be duplicated, and it is for this reason, perhaps above all others, that we must take the closest possible look at what they produced.

Yet it should not be construed that this unique resource has been neglected nor its value underestimated all these years. On the contrary, the Gettysburg photographs, like all the photographs of the Civil War, have long enjoyed the interest and appreciation of countless enthusiasts.

Being among the first and most dramatic news photographs ever taken, they were eagerly sought by the American public during the 1860s, and with little question played a significant role in shaping the nation's image of the war. Several decades after the conflict, when technological advances had finally allowed for the mass reproduction of photographs in book form, there occurred a momentous rebirth of interest in the wartime views. Publication after publication appeared on the market lavishly illustrated with hundreds, sometimes thousands, of Civil War photographs, including many of the most famous scenes of the Gettysburg battlefield. Today, heightened by both the recent Civil War centennial and the current surge of interest in all forms of early photography, public fascination with the Gettysburg series is perhaps stronger than it ever was in the past.

But despite the continued appeal of these images, their use to date as a unique source of information has been surprisingly ineffective and in numerous instances grossly inaccurate.

Traditionally, the photographs have been portrayed in one of two basic ways. They have either been presented as works of art, forced to make their own quiet and unsupported statements; or they have been placed in the secondary role of illustrations, serving the written word with varying degrees of relevance. But there is another way to look at these views. The photograph, in effect, was there. It is a historical document crying to be heard. It has a fantastic story to tell if we can only learn to provide the proper support necessary for the comprehension of its visual tale.

At first glance the task of providing such support for the Gettysburg photographs may not appear to be an unusually difficult one, for traditional captions seemingly have long given us much of the background information. Yet the time-honored captions are not what they seem to be. As will become clear, in instance after instance, they have been based, at best, on poorly researched guesswork.

Who, in fact, were the early photographers of the battlefield and from where did they come? How long after the battle were the various views taken—several days, several weeks, or several years? What portions of the field were covered by the different cameramen? What portions were neglected and why? How did each photographer interpret his subject matter? Has each photographer been properly credited with the scenes he recorded? If the currently accepted captions on the better-known Gettysburg views are incorrect, how did they come to be misidentified?

Such are the questions that must be raised and answered before we can safely feel that we are making the most fruitful use of the photographs available to us. Yet none of these questions has ever been pursued in depth. Why more research has not been performed on the Gettysburg series, a group that irrefutably contains some of the most famous historical scenes ever recorded, can only be surmised. Perhaps no one realized that more work was needed; or if anyone did, perhaps neither the tools nor the knowledge essential to execute an adequate investigation were available.

In any case, this book contains the first systematic examination of the Gettysburg series as a group, and most of the information uncovered about the photographs is presented for the first time here. In broad terms, the results of this examination should be made clear from the outset. The study does not prove, for instance, that the Civil War never actually occurred. Its conclusions are more modest, but no less satisfying. The purpose of this book, in essence, is to present the reader with a unique visual experience. By treating each photograph as an irreplaceable moment fixed in time and space, and by sharing with the reader the behind-the-scenes detective work used to document these views, I have attempted to focus on the overwhelming reality of each photograph, thereby transporting the reader back to the moment of exposure—and creating, in effect, a journey in time.

2

THE PROBLEMS OF DOCUMENTATION

In order to study any group of historical photographs effectively, it is, of course, requisite that all existing views of that particular series be examined. Although a number of early Gettysburg photographs have disappeared with the passage of time (specifically the more limited issues of F. Gutekunst and the Weavers) and remain, if at all, to be unearthed in attic trunks and obscure private collections, an impressively large number of the most important views (taken by Brady, Gardner, and the Tysons) has survived through the efforts of various public and private agencies.

In preparation for this study, I sought to uncover, to the best of my ability, every existing photograph of the Gettysburg battlefield taken between the year of the battle, 1863 (no images were ever recorded of the battle itself), and the year 1866, a span of time that includes all the significant views of the field when it looked basically as it did to the soldiers who fought there. (Additionally, interest in photographing the field declined after 1866 and would not be renewed until the 1880s.) All told, the number of early Gettysburg photographs that were examined—many in their original form of publication—exceeded two hundred and thirty.

Briefly, three items of information are necessary to document a historical scene: the name of the photographer who took the view; the date the view was taken; and an identification of the scene portrayed. Not one of these items is always as easy to document as it may seem.

Who Took the Photographs?

For many decades, Mathew Brady, Alexander Gardner, and Timothy O'Sullivan have been the photographers regularly associated with the Gettysburg battlefield. Other important figures have seldom been noted: Charles and Isaac Tyson of Gettysburg, the Weavers, Frederick Gutekunst, or Gardner's assistant James Gibson.

A great deal of confusion has long existed in establishing who worked with whom at Gettysburg and who took which photographs. Previous scholars have mistakenly attributed the vast majority, and sometimes all, of the battlefield views to the most famous of Civil War photographers, Mathew Brady. Other historians have erroneously assumed that the dramatic scenes recorded by Gardner and O'Sullivan, though properly credited, were taken under Brady's direct supervision. Similarly, little or no recognition has even been given to the Tyson brothers, primarily because of the rarity of their work today.

The difficulty currently encountered in determining the proper authorship of each photograph did not exist during the Civil War period. At the time of original issue, most photographers were careful to identify their individual firms on the label of each view. Some firms, such as Gardner's, carried these identifications one step further by giving credit to specific cameramen. Only when the great collections of Brady and Gardner negatives were mixed and reissued nearly two decades after the war, around 1880, did the original credits start to become vague. Evidently the importance of such details was not recognized by the postwar collectors, notably Albert Ordway and Arnold Rand.

In the local Gettysburg area, when Charles Tyson sold his collection of battlefield negatives, along with his studio, to William H. Tipton in 1868, Tipton proceeded to copyright all the Tyson images under his own name and continued to publish them as "photographs by Tipton" along with hundreds of his own later views. To add to this confusion, some Tyson photographs have been incorrectly attributed to Mathew Brady.

In order to determine with accuracy the source of a photograph, it was therefore necessary to study, in the original form of issue, as many Gettysburg stereographic slides, mounted prints, *cartes de visite* (small album cards), and contemporary photographic catalogues as could be uncovered (more on the popularity of this material later). Bound volumes of Civil War–period illustrated magazines were also consulted, for even though photographs as such could not be reproduced on the printed page, battle-field photographic views were occasionally printed in the form of wood-cuts, and invariably the original source was noted directly under the scene.

In some cases a characteristic common to most views in a photographer's series aided in establishing the authorship of uncredited images. One such feature was the various number sequences attached to each negative series. Brady's Gettysburg stereo views, for instance, were originally published with figures in the 2300s and 2400s; Gardner with 200s; and the Tysons with 500s. These numbers were usually scratched on the negative and appeared in a photographer's catalogue as well as on the label of the finished product. Thus, an uncredited Gettysburg negative bearing a number in the 2300s was almost assuredly taken by Brady's firm. Additional corroboratory evidence was then found by comparing the style, method of interpretation, and other distinguishing characteristics of the undocumented photograph with other photographs confirmed as the work of a particular photographer.

The precise determination of each photograph's authorship made it possible to subgroup the larger collection of views, which in turn led to further documentation.

When Were the Photographs Taken?

Because the original cameramen never specified the dates on which their Gettysburg views were taken, references to when the scenes were recorded usually—and more or less necessarily—have been either purposely vague or inadvertently false, or both. After reading a recent account of photography at Gettysburg, one gets the distinct impression that some of the cameramen were actually present during the battle, waiting behind the Union lines for temporary truce periods, at which time they apparently scurried onto the field with their cumbersome equipment, took their views, and then scurried off as the fighting resumed. While such interesting stories or suggestions provide for drama, they unfortunately contain no truth. More conscientious scholars have generally refrained from elaboration.

Indeed, if we wish to experience these historical photographs as only somewhat universal representations of man's inhumanity to man, then perhaps elaboration is unnecessary. But if, instead, we wish to regard them as irretrievable moments in time and space—as unique and so priceless documents of a specific event in our common past, the correct dating of each view must be determined as accurately as possible.

To accomplish this task, many different avenues were pursued. First of all, the images themselves were carefully examined, with particular attention being paid to datable features such as the appearance of a certain hospital, the physical condition of a rail fence, or the presence of a fallen soldier.

Obviously, a photograph of the battlefield showing a group of unburied dead had to have been taken soon after the fighting. But how soon? Questions such as this have previously been answered with unsupported guesswork, or have not been answered at all. Yet with detailed research into the burial operations at Gettysburg, it was possible to determine the timeframe during which all views showing bodies had to have been recorded.

Each scene was studied in comparison not only to other scenes by the same photographer but to the entire group of Gettysburg photographs as well. Constant comparison between views revealed many significant features, such as a change in size of a single tree or bush. These time-related features were extremely important in dating the Tysons' views for, unlike Brady or Gardner, the Tysons recorded their Gettysburg scenes over a period of several years.

Another source of information was the newspapers of the day. It was rare when a photographic firm did not advertise a new and potentially popular series. By determining the date on which a certain group of views first appeared for sale, one can reliably narrow the period in which the views must have been taken. Additionally, newspaper advertisements reflected ownership changes in the firm and studio relocations, thus providing a baseline for dating the business addresses and firm names printed on the labels of contemporary mounts.

Where Were the Scenes Taken?

The task of identifying the location and subject of each scene, which initially appeared to be a fairly simple matter, eventually proved, in a number of circumstances, to be the most frustrating and challenging aspect of the documentation attempted by this study. Interestingly enough, the difficulty of this problem was directly related to the manner in which the individual photographers chose to cover the battlefield. For example, Brady's views were the easiest to identify because of his concentration on recording

GETTYSBURG: A JOURNEY IN TIME

famous landmarks and panoramic scenes. The Tyson brothers, on the other hand, took many views in out-of-the-way portions of the battlefield and while their corresponding captions usually made reference to a general area, precise locations could be determined only by modern field investigation.

Of all the Gettysburg photographs, those taken by Gardner and his assistants presented the greatest problems in identifying the subject. Manifestly the best-known and most dramatic single group of battlefield scenes, the Gardner series has nonetheless suffered an almost continuous history of heretofore unrecognized misinterpretation. Unlike Brady, and for reasons later discussed, Gardner did not focus his attention on famous landmarks but instead chose to direct his main effort on recording close-up views of death and destruction, making an identification of the general area extremely difficult. To complicate matters, Gardner's captions for these scenes were frequently vague. As a result, the chore of providing proper identification was left to early day historians whose poorly researched assumptions had, by the turn of the century, become blindly accepted as fact.

In seeking out such identification, the value of treating photographs as part of a group, rather than as independent, unrelated items, can be seen clearly. The famous view captioned "Dead of the 24th Michigan at McPherson's Woods" (see page 205), taken by Gardner's assistant Timothy O'Sullivan, is an excellent example of this situation. Here we have a photograph showing a cluster of bodies assembled for burial in a field bordering a woodline. Viewed by itself, there is nothing in the scene that would compel one to question the authenticity of the caption. Indeed, it would seem only reasonable to assume that the person who first composed the caption had sufficient knowledge to supply as precise an identification as he did. So, in fact, have historians generally assumed and have not pursued the matter any further—not necessarily for lack of information but rather for lack of awareness that further information was required.

But by carefully examining O'Sullivan's photograph in relation to the other views of Gardner's series, curious inconsistencies emerged. It became clear that, contrary to the accepted situation, no fewer than ten views were recorded within several yards of the "24th Michigan" photograph, presumably taken at McPherson's Woods, and that the traditional captions for several of the views placed them on portions of the battlefield literally miles from the Woods. Once initial suspicions were aroused, additional contradictions, heretofore obscure, boldly demanded resolution. If these

THE PROBLEMS OF DOCUMENTATION

views were supposed to depict Union dead, why were many of the bodies in fact clothed in Confederate uniforms? Why are numerous rocks seen scattered about that particular field when none is to be found at the edge of McPherson's Woods? Once again, only through extensive modern field research could the answers to such questions be obtained.

The specific methods I employed to determine the true captions for these and other Gardner scenes are later discussed more fully.

Additional Comments

Roughly half of all the early Gettysburg photographs that I uncovered are reproduced in this work—many appearing here for the first time in book form. Views that have not been included were either repetitious in subject matter or lacking in sufficient historical interest.

In the past, a number of battlefield views have been incorrectly labeled as "taken in 1863" when they were actually taken quite a few years later. Only photographs taken prior to the end of 1866 will be found in this book.

Needless to say, not all the many questions that surround the Gettysburg series have been completely answered. This fact will become readily apparent as the reader progresses. Not all the views have been located precisely. Not all the credits have been established nor the exact dates fixed. But where important questions have not been adequately answered, they have been so noted and the possible reasons are discussed in either the main text or in the respective captions.

PART TWO
THE PHOTOGRAPHERS AT GETTYSBURG

3

GARDNER AND HIS MEN

The Journey to Gettysburg

The first photographers to descend upon the Gettysburg battlefield were Alexander Gardner, Timothy H. O'Sullivan and James F. Gibson. They produced nearly sixty negatives.[1]

Alexander Gardner, the leader of the group and a pioneer of wet plate photography, had emigrated from Scotland to the United States in 1856 and two years later was managing the Washington branch of Mathew Brady's photographic gallery. By May of 1863, however, Gardner had terminated his association with the famous Brady and succeeded in establishing his own Washington studio.

Gardner was substantially more effective than Brady in dealing with employees and was quickly able to attract two other former Brady assistants, Timothy H. O'Sullivan, who is currently recognized as one of the finest field photographers to cover the Civil War, and James F. Gibson.

Whether all three men were together in Washington when the early reports of the battle electrified that city on July 3, two days after the battle had begun, is not known; but since all three were present when the first photographs were recorded on the battlefield a short while later, it is safe

GETTYSBURG: A JOURNEY IN TIME

to assume that they traveled the seventy-seven miles from Washington to Gettysburg as a unit. The possibility exists that a rendezvous occurred somewhere along the route, but considering communication difficulties and the short period of time that elapsed before actual work was begun, the achievement of such delicate coordination seems exceedingly remote. In fact, judging from Gardner's speed in responding to the early reports of fighting, it is quite conceivable that he and his assistants had been prepared to move for several days.

One of the most important clues in accurately establishing when Gardner conducted his journey to Gettysburg—important as a basic step in dating his work there—is the caption on his stereoscopic slide entitled "Farmer's Inn and Hotel, Emmitsburg, where our Special Artist was captured, July 5, 1863."[2] (The view itself was not taken until July 7 or 8.)

Left, Alexander Gardner, sketch by the author

Right, Timothy H. O'Sullivan, stereo self-portrait taken in Panama, 1870 (NA)*

* For explanation of the caption data, see pp. 58–59.

The caption is very likely an accurate one. Emmitsburg, Maryland, situated approximately ten miles southwest of Gettysburg along the direct
route from Washington, was indeed the scene of a minor incident two days
following the battle. Confederate General J. E. B. Stuart mentioned in his
official report of the Pennsylvania Campaign that on July 5, at about dawn,
his cavalry rode into Emmitsburg and halted for a short while, capturing
a number of Union soldiers and a quantity of sorely needed medical supplies.

According to the caption, only one of the three cameramen was detained
by the Confederates at the Farmer's Inn, suggesting that the other two were
elsewhere when the raid occurred. (A possible explanation for this temporary separation is that, as chance would have it, Gardner's fifteen-year-old
son, Lawrence, was attending boarding school on the outskirts of Emmitsburg that year,[3] and it is plausible to suggest that the boy's father, accompanied by one of his assistants, was insuring his son's safety at the time.)
In any case, whichever cameraman was detained, it is doubtful that his

"capture" consisted of more than a brief interrogation and subsequent release, for the photographers possessed nothing of military value.

Anxious to reach their final destination, Gardner and his assistants would not have lingered in Maryland any longer than was absolutely necessary, and from all the available information it seems that sometime on the morning of July 5 (the so-called capture took place at dawn), they embarked on the last leg of their trek northward.

Because road conditions between Emmitsburg and Gettysburg had deteriorated as a result of the unusually heavy rains which followed the battle, two hours would be a conservative estimate for the length of time it took the cameramen to cover the remaining distance of their journey. Assuming, therefore, that Gardner, O'Sullivan, and Gibson began recording scenes shortly after their arrival on the battlefield, their first photographs at Gettysburg were probably taken, at the earliest, sometime in the late morning, and prior to noon, on July 5, 1863.

Preoccupation with the Dead

Of the approximately sixty negatives produced by the Gardner team at Gettysburg, almost 75 percent contain as their main subject matter bloated corpses, open graves, dead horses, and related details of wholesale carnage. It is by no means an overstatement to conclude that Gardner's prime concern was to record the horrors of war rather than the area's landmarks (prominent features, man-made or natural) or general views of the terrain. This fascination with the dead on the part of Gardner is of more than passing interest because it determined, in effect, that those areas bearing the ugliest scars would receive the greatest attention from the first cameramen to reach the field.

The reason for Gardner's preoccupation with the dead becomes clear when the fame of his earlier work in the Civil War is reviewed. In September 1862 Gardner took a series of views showing the Antietam battlefield prior to the completion of burial operations. Since most Americans in 1862 had never before seen an actual photograph of battlefield dead, the emotional response these scenes engendered was great.

Articles on the views were run by both the *New York Times* and *Harper's Weekly*, the latter reproducing several scenes in the form of woodcut engravings.[4] Dr. Oliver Wendell Holmes, who had recently returned from Antietam in search of his wounded son, wrote of the photographs in a contemporary issue of *Atlantic Monthly* (July 1863):

Let him who wishes to know what war is look at this series of illustrations. . . . It was so nearly like visiting the battlefield to look over these views, that all the emotions excited by the actual sight of the stained and sordid scene, strewed with rags and wrecks, came back to us, and we buried them in the recesses of our cabinet as we would have buried the mutilated remains of the dead they too vividly represented. . . . The sight of these pictures is a commentary on civilization such as the savage might well triumph to show its missionaries.[5]

The popularity of photographs of the dead during the Civil War is also evident from the fact that few modern collections of original Civil War stereoscopic slides are without a number of examples.

Considering both the rapidity with which Gardner and his men reached the Gettysburg battlefield and the type of view they spent most of their time taking, it is apparent that Gardner was fully aware of the potential market value such views possessed. But to repeat his earlier success, Gardner had to work swiftly, for by the early afternoon of July 5, Union burial details at Gettysburg had made significant headway in covering the ugliest battle scars. Fortunately for the cameramen, their approach to Gettysburg via the Emmitsburg Road placed them immediately upon one of the last portions of the battlefield to be cleared of its dead, the area near the Rose farm.

Photographing the Battlefield

Before attempting to reconstruct Gardner's actual work at Gettysburg, it is necessary as a preliminary step to take a closer look at some of the technical factors that influenced his manner of operation. One such factor concerned the use of the negative.

Although most Civil War–period photographers were well aware that different-sized print enlargements could be made from one negative, the contemporary methods of enlargement were still primitive and impractical, and were rarely employed. Instead, finished photographic prints were all but universally produced through direct contact with the negative. Thus, if a firm desired to offer its customers prints in varying sizes and formats, then correspondingly different negatives had to be used.

To achieve this variety in his Gettysburg series, Gardner utilized the two basic cameras of his day: a large single plate camera equipped to handle eight-by-ten-inch glass negatives, and a stereo camera which produced a double image on a smaller glass negative. As far as open air photography was concerned, Gardner's greatest source of income was derived from the sale of stereo slides, and consequently some 80 percent of his entire Gettysburg series was recorded with the twin-lensed stereo camera. The resulting double negatives were also used to print single *cartes de visite*, but generally these were not as popular as the three-dimensional slides.

Another important technical factor was the method by which the negative was prepared and developed. To produce their battlefield series, Civil War photographers, without exception, employed the wet plate process. Briefly, this process first required that the photographer, on location and within the confines of a portable darkroom, pour a syrupy solution, known as collodion, over a meticulously cleaned glass plate. After draining off the excess liquid, the coating, which had to be perfectly uniform, was allowed to become tacky, but not dry, whereupon the plate was bathed in a chemical solution rendering the emulsion light sensitive. This collodion-covered plate then became what is today known as the "film." At this point, the plate was carefully placed in a light-proof holder and rushed from the darkroom to the nearby camera. Immediately following exposure the plate was returned to the portable darkroom for its development. At no time during the process, from first step to last, could the solution on the plate become dry, for dampness was vital to the light sensitivity of the chemicals. With Gardner and his experienced employees working together as a team, this entire procedure would have taken approximately ten minutes per plate.[6]

Although the exact work pattern of the three men is uncertain, a study of the credits in Gardner's 1863 catalogue reveals that all three took turns recording the stereo scenes, each man being credited with one third of those views. O'Sullivan, on the other hand, was the exclusive operator of the less-often-used single plate camera.[7]

Whether or not Gardner's crew was accompanied by additional darkroom assistants is unknown, but the possibility clearly exists that the photographers themselves periodically rotated job functions and performed the task of processing negatives when not engaged at the camera. An examination of Gardner's scenes indicates that two darkroom wagons were present at Gettysburg (II-12, VI-4 and 5),* and while it is pure speculation, I would

---

* Each photograph is designated by a Roman numeral, which identifies its battlefield area, and a second number, which places it within the area group. For example, VI-3 means group VI (The Rose farm), scene number three.

suggest that Gardner may have used one wagon for plate sensitization and the other for development, thereby increasing the efficiency of his darkroom support.

A third technical aspect of photography which should be discussed is lighting and its effect on the exposed wet plate negative. Unlike modern high-speed films, the sensitivity of the Civil War–period plate was extremely low. Given sufficient sunlight, the wet plate photographer, with his camera mounted on a sturdy tripod, could only hope to realize an average exposure time, at best, of approximately five or ten seconds. Obviously, any motion in a scene was a distinct handicap, for even the slightest movement, such as the ruffle of a tree in the wind, produced a noticeable blur on the finished plate. Yet the complete avoidance of all motion was many times impossible and to at least minimize the effect of this handicap, the photographer had to rely heavily on the presence of adequate sunlight to obtain the shortest exposure time possible. In addition, effective lighting conditions were of paramount importance for the achievement of high quality, sharp detail, and well-balanced contrast.

It is therefore not surprising, when the shadows in Gardner's Gettysburg scenes are analyzed, to discover that he refrained from taking photographs in the early morning or late afternoon, choosing instead to record almost all his views when the sun was fairly high in the sky, roughly between the hours of 10:00 A.M. and 4:00 or 5:00 P.M.

But even this apparently self-imposed time limitation did not insure consistent quality throughout the Gardner series. The weather following the battle was far from ideal. Frequent showers and the subsequent mist they produced interrupted the photographically necessary periods of sunshine, affecting, in more than one instance, the clarity of Gardner's backgrounds, which were often hazy and indistinct.

Now, by considering all such factors which might have influenced Gardner's work pattern at Gettysburg, it becomes possible to reconstruct his movements across the field with a fair degree of accuracy. For example, if we coordinate the approximate time the photographers initiated their work at Gettysburg with the total number of views they took, with the time of day the views were recorded, with the amount of time it required to make a single plate, with the geographic areas in which the cameramen worked, with the distance and terrain between areas, and finally with such factors as the date on which the last bodies on the field were buried, a conjectural itinerary pattern emerges.

According to available evidence, the task of burying the dead on the battlefield proper was for all practical purposes completed by the night of July 6.[8] If Gardner, therefore, desired a significant number of photographs showing corpses, which he plainly did, he would not have had time to explore the twenty-five square miles surrounding Gettysburg in quest of specific subjects. Undoubtedly his first photographs recorded on July 5 were those taken of the still-large concentration of bodies initially encountered in the southern extremity of the battlefield near the Rose farm, an area within sight of the Emmitsburg Road.

Approximately twenty negatives were produced in this vicinity, and allowing for the time it took to move both the men and their assemblage of fragile equipment from one area to another, considered together with the roughly ten-minute time period required to process each plate, plus the time required to select and compose their views, it becomes clear that the greater part of the first afternoon must have been expended in the Rose farm area. Considering also that few, if any, of Gardner's scenes were photographed beyond 4:00 or 5:00 P.M., it is relatively safe to assume that once the cameramen had finished their work in the vicinity of the Rose farm, the remaining daylight hours of July 5 were devoted to searching for the next day's subject matter.

Traveling northward along the Emmitsburg Road for a short distance, then eastward by way of the Wheatfield Road and then southward through the Valley of Death, Gardner eventually came upon the awesome group of rock formations known as Devil's Den. The compositional possibilities presented by this wild and fascinating scene must have caused great excitement among the cameramen, whose work until then had been primarily limited to open fields.

Probably camping in close proximity to the Den on the night of July 5, the photographers resumed their labors sometime on the morning of July 6, beginning their work in Devil's Den. They would record the bulk of their Gettysburg series this day. Many of these Devil's Den scenes were taken in what the cameramen identified as the "Slaughter Pen," a shallow ravine bordered on the west by the Den and on the east by the wooded base of Big Round Top.

The views recorded in the Den area on the morning and early afternoon of July 6 were the last of Gardner's Gettysburg scenes depicting human corpses. In fact, the sixteen different bodies photographed in the Den were probably among the last to remain unburied on the entire field. In any case, an abrupt termination to this type of photograph occurs with the cameramen's departure from the vicinity.*

Turning their attention eastward, the three cameramen apparently were immediately attracted by the imposing sight of Little Round Top. Three views of the hill were taken from the edge of Devil's Den and eight more were completed on the summit. Because of atmospheric conditions, however, the cameramen could not capitalize on the panoramic scenes that Little Round Top afforded and, instead, contented themselves with composing studies of the stone breastworks constructed by Union forces during the battle.

Comparatively few scenes were recorded after the cameramen ventured forth from the southern portion of the field. From Little Round Top they traveled northward toward the town of Gettysburg, halting to photograph the Trostle farmyard and the small building used by Union General Meade as his headquarters during the battle. Dead horses were everywhere and one can only imagine with disgust the pungent odors that must have confronted Gardner, O'Sullivan, and Gibson as they journeyed across the field. These images were most likely recorded during the afternoon of the sixth.

A study of the shadows in O'Sullivan's photograph of the gateway to Evergreen Cemetery (II-8), which lay just outside the town, reveals that the view was taken at approximately 11:00 A.M., suggesting that the cameramen camped near the cemetery on the night of July 6, and resumed their work in that area on the morning of July 7. Several photographs, including an excellent scene of the town, were produced from this locale.

The final photographs taken by the Gardner crew were two views of the United States Sanitary Commission headquarters, in Gettysburg itself. The structure (Fahnestock's clothing store on Baltimore Street) was not occupied by the Sanitary Commission before July 7 (I-15).

When one reflects upon the odd nature of this, the only known Gardner

---

* A number of Gardner views showing fallen soldiers have traditionally been identified as scenes taken on the first day's battlefield but extensive field investigation and related research do not support these assertions.

subject photographed in the town itself, it becomes apparent that Gardner and his assistants must have regarded their work at Gettysburg complete once they reached the borough streets. That they would have stopped photographing at that point when so many significant and impressive features, such as the Lutheran Theological Seminary, lay but a short distance to the west is strange, but perhaps explicable, given Gardner's interests and his lack of familiarity with the battlefield.

Thus having terminated their work at Gettysburg sometime in the early afternoon of July 7, Gardner and his crew commenced their long journey back to Washington. They had, in effect, scooped all potential competitors.

Once again passing through Emmitsburg, they halted for a short while to produce a series of seven negatives, including, of course, a view of the Farmer's Inn which had figured so prominently in their adventure. These Emmitsburg views indicate that the three photographers had not exhausted their supply of negatives while at Gettysburg.

Evaluation of Gardner's Work

In considering the work accomplished by Gardner, O'Sullivan, and Gibson on the Gettysburg battlefield, we come to the curious fact that in terms of geographic variety and in the number of landmarks photographed, Gardner and his men did not cover the field well. Why they did not photograph such subjects as Lee's headquarters, Pennsylvania College, the Lutheran Seminary, or the Union breastworks on Culp's Hill, all favorite subjects of later photographers, will never be known for sure. Admittedly, Gardner's prime interest in the battlefield centered on the dead and possibly because this concern was satisfied on the southern extreme of the field (or rather eliminated by the completion of burial operations), all subsequent subjects may have seemed anti-climactic by comparison. But why then would he have expended two negatives on the relatively dull Sanitary Commission headquarters while neglecting to photograph the highly imposing Lutheran Seminary?

One conclusion is that Gardner's greatest advantage was also his greatest handicap. He simply arrived on the battlefield too soon after the fighting. The town itself was still recovering from the shock of war and few, if any, people, civilian or military, had had time to reconstruct the confused events which had just taken place. Gardner could not have had a competent guide, for none was available at that early date. Indeed, judging from the areas his group covered, it appears that the cameramen wandered across the battlefield by themselves, asking questions as they progressed.

It is frustrating today to consider the many scenes that could have been taken by Gardner and never were. On the other hand, Gardner's views are unique in several respects. Gardner, O'Sullivan, and Gibson were the only early photographers to record the extreme southern portion of the battlefield, south and west of the Rose Woods on the Rose property. They were the only men to photograph the battlefield while its dead still lay exposed, revealing, as only a photograph can, the true horrors of Gettysburg. And finally, Gardner's views are the earliest in existence that show the field as it basically looked to the soldiers who fought there during the first three days of July 1863.

4

MATHEW BRADY

Soon after the departure of Alexander Gardner, Timothy O'Sullivan, and James Gibson from Gettysburg, a second group of photographers, led by the distinguished Mathew Brady, arrived upon the battlefield.

Brady, like Gardner, had maintained a keen interest in the creation of a photographic record of the Civil War. In fact, without Brady's initial efforts in mobilizing a professional force of field photographers in 1861, it is doubtful that battlefields such as Gettysburg would have been covered to the extent that they were.[9]

Brady was the owner of two galleries in 1863, one in New York and the other in Washington, D.C., and while it cannot be established for certain where he was at the time of the battle, it appears most likely that he was in Manhattan when he first learned of the fighting at Gettysburg. It took Brady a longer time than it did Gardner to reach the field, and Brady had always been more closely associated with his New York gallery than with the gallery in Washington.

Dating the Brady Series

There is little question that Brady's series was executed within at least a month following the battle, for eleven of his views were published as

Mathew B. Brady,
Brady Studio,
probably cdv, ca.
1863 (NA)

woodcuts in an August 1863 issue of *Harper's Weekly*.[10] On the other hand, it is also fairly evident that Brady's views were recorded subsequent to Gardner's departure from the field, because none of Brady's approximately thirty scenes reveals the presence of human dead. Brady, as much as any other photographer, would have been acutely aware of the sales potential such views possessed. It can only be concluded that his arrival upon the field occurred sometime after July 6, the date on which the last of the battlefield dead were buried.

GETTYSBURG: A JOURNEY IN TIME

Yet a comparison between Brady and Gardner images of the same subject indicates that the time between them was not very great. In a Gardner view recorded on Little Round Top (V-6), for example, a rail of some sort may be seen propped against the low branches of a young pine tree. A Brady view taken by coincidence from almost the identical location (V-7) shows the same rail in the same position. This is not to say that the rail could not have remained undisturbed for quite some time, but considering the number of tourists, small boys, and relic hunters who flocked over the field immediately after the battle, it is doubtful that even a rail oddly propped against a tree would have remained undisturbed for long. This consideration aside, a more precise, though speculative, delineation of when Brady visited the battlefield is obtainable through a closer examination of his scenes.

In the distant background of Brady's panoramic photograph taken from near the Lutheran Seminary (1-7), several tents may be detected on the far side of town at the site of Camp Letterman, a huge consolidated hospital established to replace the various temporary field hospitals scattered about the Gettysburg area. Although the specific dates of Camp Letterman's construction are unknown, an analysis of the official case histories of numerous wounded soldiers reveals that at least a portion of the camp was already receiving its first patients by and possibly slightly prior to July 23.[11]

Taking into account the fact that the tents in Brady's view were probably erected before the camp was actually in operating condition, or during the period when supplies were being transferred, woods cleared, and drainage and sanitary facilities constructed, it is reasonable to assume that this photograph could have been taken during the preparatory phase that occurred sometime in the third week of July, or roughly between July 15 and July 21. It is extremely unlikely that any tents (at the site of Camp Letterman) would have appeared in Brady's photograph had it been taken much prior to July 15.

A frequently reproduced Brady photograph taken near the Seminary depicts three Confederate prisoners posing beside some log breastworks (I-5). Since one of the last, if not *the* last, group of such able-bodied prisoners was removed from the Gettysburg area on July 16, it is correspondingly doubtful that this photograph was recorded subsequent to that date.[12] Thus it appears that Brady could not have been on Seminary Ridge much prior to July 15 and probably not after July 16.

Perhaps the most significant piece of evidence in determining the dates of Brady's series is the handwritten caption on one of his photographs currently on display at the Lee's Headquarters Museum in Gettysburg. The caption reads: "General R. E. Lee's personal headquarters . . . picture taken July 15, 1863." Although the author of the caption is unknown and the caption itself appears to have been written sometime after the war, there is little reason to doubt its accuracy, for if a person were deliberately attaching a false date to the photograph, the chances are great that he would have made the date closer to the battle.

Thus, since July 15 is indeed about the approximate time of Brady's presence on the battlefield, it will be assumed for the purpose of this study that Brady took his Gettysburg views during several days beginning either on or about July 15, or approximately one week to a week and a half after Gardner left the field.

Photographing the Battlefield

Inasmuch as Brady arrived on the battlefield too late to record scenes of carnage such as those taken by the Gardner team, his attention, as evidenced by his photographs, was focused on significant landmarks and general views of the terrain. Possibly two or three days were expended by the Brady team in completing its series of some thirty views which included both eight-by-ten-inch plates and the more lucrative stereographic negatives.[13]

Because Brady, unlike Gardner, did not credit each photograph with the name of a photographer, it is virtually impossible to identify his assistant cameramen or to reconstruct a work pattern similar to that created for the Gardner crew. It is fairly certain, however, that none of the views was personally taken by Brady. Failing eyesight had long precluded him from operating a camera, and the famous photographer's role at Gettysburg was essentially that of a supervisor.[14] Of some significance is the varying presence of at least one of three men in most of the Brady views. The three consist of Brady and two men who no doubt were his assistants, one wearing a dark vest, the other a white shirt occasionally covered by a white duster. A view taken near Little Round Top (V-1) shows all three men together, which indicates the presence of another companion operating the camera. Whether or not this third assistant took most or all of the photographs cannot be determined.

As far as working conditions were concerned, the Brady team was considerably more fortunate than the Gardner team had been. The basic advantage lay in the fact that Brady was not forced to contend with the problem of rapid burial operations, since these had already terminated. Periods of rainy weather continued throughout the month of July, but the absence of time pressure allowed Brady to record his scenes whenever atmospheric conditions were at their best. The consistently sharp, detailed backgrounds that characterize his photographs testify not only to Brady's skill but also to the circumstances under which he worked.

A review of the landmarks covered by the Brady team indicates that a guide accompanied the cameramen over the field; and while it is impossible to establish a chronological itinerary without knowledge of the various time elements involved, we can at least follow Brady from one point to another. Unlike the Gardner series, Brady's photographs are quite easy to identify by the subjects they recorded: McPherson's Woods, Lee's headquarters, the Lutheran Seminary, Pennsylvania College, the town of Gettysburg, John Burns at his home, the breastworks on Culp's Hill, the cemetery gateway, the Bryan house (incorrectly identified by Brady as Meade's headquarters), and finally Little Round Top, with the expansive northward view afforded from the hill's summit.

Evaluation of Brady's Work at Gettysburg

Brady's photographs, though lacking the dramatic impact of Gardner's series, nevertheless serve as an invaluable and unique guide to the field's appearance during the month of the battle. Brady chose to interpret his subject matter in a somber and bucolic manner, strongly reflecting the influence of nineteenth-century romantic thought. Little evidence of wholesale destruction, aside from damaged fences, disturbed the serene mood of his composition. One or two lone assistants were frequently posed gazing off toward the distant fields and woods as if contemplating the awesome events of two weeks before. Recording only half the number of scenes his predecessor did, Brady's heavier concentration on sweeping panoramas and subjects of general historical interest provides sufficient compensation for any numerical difference.

Unfortunately, as with Gardner, several frustrating gaps occur in Brady's itinerary at Gettysburg. Among those areas the second group of photographers neglected are the "High Water Mark," the Peach Orchard, the Wheatfield, and oddly enough Devil's Den, which Brady could not have helped but notice from the summit of Little Round Top. Perhaps the boulders of the Den did not seem quite as impressive without their dead. We can only assume that Brady was unaware of the fame these particular features possessed, or otherwise considered them to be inferior subjects from a strictly photographic standpoint.

Because Brady's work at Gettysburg has never before been adequately distinguished from the work of Gardner, O'Sullivan, and Gibson, and because Brady's name has long dominated the history of Civil War photography, many more scenes have traditionally been credited to the famed photographer than he actually took or supervised. But even when his work is placed in proper perspective, we are left with a deep sense of appreciation for his efforts and accomplishments on the battlefield. His irreplaceable series of photographic documents will forever play an integral role in the interpretation of our nation's tragic experience at Gettysburg.

5

THE TYSON BROTHERS

At first, it might seem unusual that the town of Gettysburg, which had its own established photographers long before the battle, did not produce the first cameraman to photograph the field. In fact, Charles and Isaac Tyson, owners of Gettysburg's Excelsior Gallery since 1859, were possibly two weeks behind Brady in taking their first views.[15]

The reasons for this delay become apparent when one examines the nature of the Excelsior Gallery. Being a relatively small-scale operation which catered primarily to a localized portrait trade, the Tyson firm, known officially as "Tyson Brothers" until 1865, lacked both the portable equipment and much of the experience necessary for wet plate field photography. There simply had been no large demand for outdoor views in the Gettysburg area before the battle, and to the author's knowledge, few, if any, photographs had ever been recorded of the town or its immediate vicinity prior to July 1863.

The Tyson gallery oddly enough remained open during the first few hours of the battle, as throngs of Union soldiers rushed to have their likenesses made. When the capture of Gettysburg by Southern forces appeared imminent, Charles Tyson locked the gallery and fled from the town with his

Isaac G. (left) and Charles J. Tyson, Tyson Studio, cdv, ca. 1864 (Tyson)

wife. Upon his return several days after the battle, the studio and all its equipment were found undamaged. A Confederate artillery shell which had struck the Tyson building under one of the second story windows failed to explode.[16] The shell may still be seen there today.

Although it is not known exactly how soon after the battle Charles and Isaac Tyson first realized the sales potential that views of the battlefield would have, most of their delay in beginning work was probably caused by the necessary adjustment from studio to field photography.

The Early Series

On August 10, 1863, the Tyson brothers announced to the public that "a series of splendid photographic views of all the prominent points of interest upon the battle-field of Gettysburg" was then "in preparation" and would soon be completed.[17]

This first Tyson series consisted of no fewer than eighteen different views in the eight-by-ten-inch format. The work on this group was probably begun sometime near the end of July or more likely the beginning of August, approximately one month after the battle. There is nothing in the views themselves that suggests they were taken any earlier. Furthermore, since Camp Letterman, recorded in full operation by the Tysons, complete with elaborate ornaments and decorations, was not so operating until the beginning of August (and since the Camp appears in at least eight of the photographs), it is relatively safe to assume that most of the views, especially in light of the newspaper announcement, were taken in August 1863.

Curiously, much of the work produced by Charles and Isaac Tyson on the field bears a striking resemblance to the Gettysburg views of Mathew Brady. The subject selection, camera positions, general composition, and even the style of many Tyson views are so similar to corresponding views in Brady's series that the possibility exists—though the suggestion of course is purely conjectural—that perhaps one or both of the Tyson brothers accompanied or even assisted the famous photographer as he toured the field.

An examination of the scenes portrayed by the Tysons in their eight-by-ten-inch series, which duplicated the earlier work of Mathew Brady, reveals that the quality of the Tyson views was often equal to Brady's. Nevertheless, from a business standpoint the similarity has little consequence since the brothers were not in direct competition with the city photographers, the Tyson market having been primarily centered on the tourist and local trade.

At the same time that Charles and Isaac were recording their series of eight-by-ten-inch views, they also produced an unknown number of smaller album card photographs. I have seen eight different cards with the imprint of "Tyson Brothers" on the back, including four views taken at Camp Letterman, which would support the fact that these cards were also made in 1863. Only one of the eight views, an image showing the cemetery gate, appears to have been taken later, possibly in 1864 (II–10).

The Stereo Series

In addition to the eight-by-ten-inch plates and the album cards, the Tysons produced a stereographic series of approximately one hundred views. To determine when the series was taken, it is essential to examine briefly the history of the Tyson firm in the years after the battle.

The General
Hospital at Camp
Letterman, View
looking West
toward
Gettysburg,
Tyson, plate,
August 1863 (LC)

U. S. Sanitary
Commission
Headquarters at
Camp Letterman,
Tyson, plate,
August 1863 (LC)

In November 1865, Charles Tyson sold his share of the business to his brother, Isaac, who changed the name of the gallery to "Isaac G. Tyson, successor to Tyson Brothers." Running the firm for approximately one year, Isaac decided, late in 1866, to leave Gettysburg and open a studio in Philadelphia. In December of that year, Charles Tyson bought back the entire business. His growing interest in nurseries, however, frequently took Charles from the gallery until finally in October 1868, he sold the business to two of his assistants, William H. Tipton and Robert Myers.

The dates of Charles J. Tyson's sole ownership (December 1866 to October 1868) are extremely important in light of the fact that every Tyson stereograph personally examined by the author and included in this study was published under the C. J. Tyson label. Although these particular views could not have been issued before December 1866, when C. J. became the sole owner and proprietor of the firm, it is nonetheless apparent, based on the following evidence, that most of the negatives were actually taken between 1864 and the summer of 1866.

The first newspaper advertisement to mention the Tyson stereo series of the battlefield appeared in January 1867, less than one month after Charles Tyson assumed ownership of the gallery.[18] Since most of the views bearing the imprint of C. J. Tyson were obviously taken in the summer months, the negatives for the series advertised in January 1867 had to have been recorded no later than the summer of 1866.

The reliably reported, though otherwise unconfirmable existence of a "Tyson Brothers" catalogue listing over one hundred stereographs of Gettysburg and vicinity suggests that a good many, if not most or all of the negatives which C. J. Tyson used for his issue of 1867 were recorded prior to the break-up of the partnership in 1865.[19] (The practice of using the same negatives year after year was quite common, especially during the days of wet plate photography. In fact, many of the Tyson views taken during the 1860s were still being published by William Tipton more than twenty years later.) Judging from the physical appearance of the scenes represented by the Tyson stereos, that is the size of certain trees, bushes, the absence or presence of certain buildings, etc., all of the views that may be considered datable appear to have been taken at least a year or two after the battle and no earlier.

Indeed, it is my belief that the Tysons took few, if any, stereo views on the field before 1864, and if, by supposition, a number of stereographic scenes were made in 1863, then traces of this important series had all but vanished by the time of C. J. Tyson's reissue in January 1867. The Tyson brothers apparently concentrated most of their efforts of 1863 on the production of the eight-by-ten-inch series and album cards rather than stereographic slides. It is reasonably safe to conclude, therefore, that most of the Tyson stereos, or at least most of those examined and presented in this study, were taken between 1864 and 1866, or more simply circa 1865.

Evaluation of the Tysons' Work

When comparing the earlier eight-by-ten-inch and album card views with the later stereographic series, several significant differences in subject content and style are readily observed. While the earlier views were, for the most part, scenes of prominent features and landmarks of historic interest taken from well-chosen perspectives, roughly half of the stereo series may be classified as nature studies, that is, close-ups of rocks and woods. In this half of the series, the constant repetition of subject type and the overwhelming emphasis on nature studies in the Culp's Hill and Devil's Den areas are truly disappointing to the student of the battle.

Perhaps the Tysons felt that such studies were better adapted to three-dimensional viewing than were the more sweeping scenes of general interest; or perhaps they simply decided to interpret the field as a romantic wilderness rather than a historic area to be documented.

Fortunately for the historian, however, the other half of the Tyson stereograph series contains many fine views of buildings and areas that no other photographer covered. Included are the earliest and rarest views of Willoughby's Run, public buildings, churches, Rock Creek, Spangler's Meadow, and the interior of Evergreen Cemetery.

Largely overlooked by historians, the Tysons' photographs, when added to the collections of Gardner and Brady, produce an amazingly well-balanced documentation of the Gettysburg battlefield as it appeared during the 1860s (despite the several significant and frustrating gaps common to all three collections: the field of Pickett's charge, the Peach Orchard, the Wheatfield, etc.). It is one of the purposes of this study, therefore, that a long overdue recognition at last be given to the efforts and accomplishments of Charles and Isaac Tyson.

6

ADDITIONAL PHOTOGRAPHERS

While most of the best and earliest views of the Gettysburg battlefield to survive were taken by the Gardner and Brady teams and by the Tyson brothers, these photographers were by no means the only cameramen to cover the field between 1863 and 1866. The most important of the other figures are briefly mentioned here.

Frederick Gutekunst

Gutekunst, a prominent Philadelphia photographer, visited the field within three weeks after the battle and took seven ten-by-twelve-inch views. They included Meade's headquarters, the field of the first day's battle, Union positions looking east from Evergreen Cemetery, the Seminary, John Burns's home, and the Second Corps hospital, the latter view being the only one I have been able to uncover. Mention of this numerically small and now extremely rare set was first made on July 23, 1863, in an advertisement in the *Philadelphia Inquirer*. The views were to "be sold by subscription only;

the proceeds of sales to be used for the benefit of our sick and wounded soldiers.'' The price for the entire set was ten dollars.

Peter S. and Hanson E. Weaver

The Weavers of Hanover, Pennsylvania, twelve miles east of Gettysburg, were quick to respond to the photographic possibilities of the battlefield. There is little question that they were on the field in 1863, perhaps as early as mid-July. At least five of their larger plate scenes are known to have been recorded at Camp Letterman, which was disbanded after three months. When their "Gems around the Battlefield" series of approximately eighty-five stereo views was recorded is less certain. I have seen only twenty-six views from this series, all of which appear to have been produced within a year or two of the battle.[20] Like the Tyson brothers, the Weavers concentrated heavily on stereographic nature studies of rocks and trees.

According to a letter written by one of the Weavers stating that he photographed the dedication ceremonies at which Lincoln spoke (November 19, 1863), it is quite conceivable that a number of the still uncredited scenes taken that day were recorded by their firm.[21] (Alexander Gardner made brief reference in his *Sketch Book* to having attended the November 1863 dedication ceremonies. The general unreliability of the caption/stories in that work, however, casts serious doubt on his claim.)[22] Additionally, a Weaver series of *cartes de visite* of live soldiers posing as dead men in Devil's Den shows trees that are bare (V–22), which suggests that if the Weavers were in Gettysburg in November 1863, both series may have been produced then. This would also explain where the photographers located the soldiers to pose for them at that time.

Others

There are still several important views of the battlefield, some of which were obviously taken within weeks of the fighting, that cannot be definitely credited to any single photographer or group of photographers. A cameraman was known to have accompanied Dr. John H. Brinton of the Army Medical Department on his trip to Gettysburg soon after the battle. The photographer's primary mission was to produce a series of photographs documenting the various types of wounds received by soldiers during the fight. It is possible that several uncredited scenes were taken by this unidentified cameraman.[23]

The story of photography at Gettysburg, even during the period before

The Union
Second Corps
Hospital, Rock
Creek, Gutekunst,
plate, July 1863
(NPS)

William H. Tipton
and the Tyson
Darkroom Wagon,
photographed at
Meade's
Headquarters,
Tyson, cdv, ca.
1863 (Tyson)

ADDITIONAL PHOTOGRAPHERS

1866, would not be complete without brief mention of the work of William H. Tipton. Employed by the Tyson brothers as a twelve-year-old apprentice at the time of the battle, young Tipton was eventually to become sole owner of the Gettysburg gallery and without doubt the most important photographer of the Gettysburg battlefield during the last third of the nineteenth century. His collection of glass plate negatives, containing many taken by the Tyson brothers, is today preserved at the National Archives.[24]

PART THREE

THE
PHOTOGRAPHS

7

THE BATTLE OF GETTYSBURG

For the first two years of fighting, the Civil War (1861–1865) went well for the South. After a temporary setback at Antietam, Maryland (September 1862), the Confederate Army of Northern Virginia, commanded by General Robert E. Lee, went on to win two decisive victories at Fredericksburg, Virginia (December 1862) and Chancellorsville, Virginia (May 1863). Emboldened by success, Lee decided to bring the war into enemy territory. At no other time during the entire four years of fighting was the South closer to total victory than it was in June 1863, when Lee began his move. The Lincoln Administration, tempered by its army's defeat, was coming under increasing pressure to capitulate.

On June 3, 1863, Lee's Army of Northern Viriginia started northward via the Shenandoah and Cumberland valleys. The Union Army of the Potomac, whose commander, Major General Joseph Hooker, was replaced in desperation at the last moment with Major General George G. Meade, followed the invaders, traveling east of the mountains. Because large amounts of men and equipment had to be moved over great distances, both armies were fairly dispersed by the end of June. But basically the Confederate army was located

GETTYSBURG: A JOURNEY IN TIME

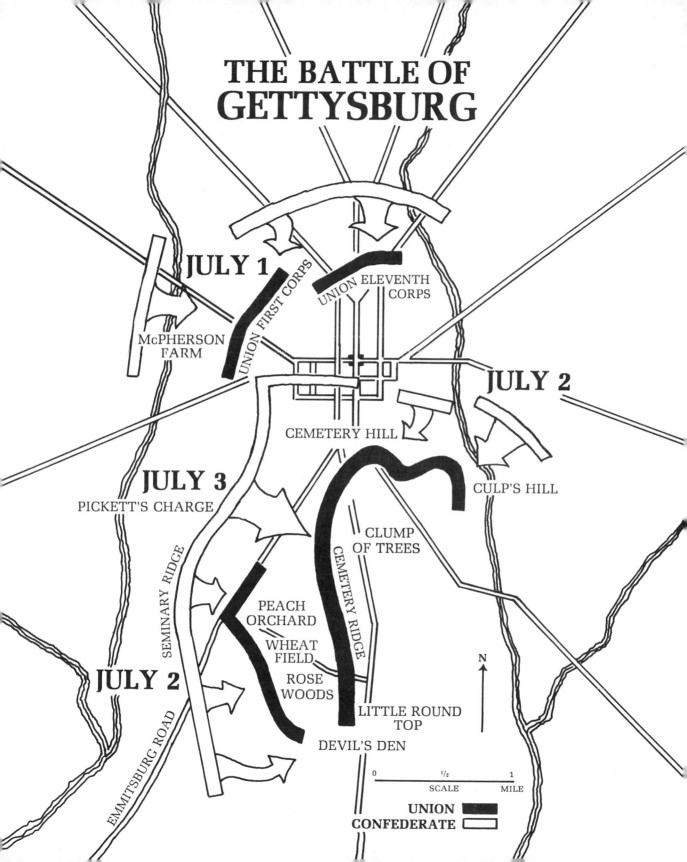

THE BATTLE OF GETTYSBURG

JULY 1

McPHERSON FARM

UNION FIRST CORPS

UNION ELEVENTH CORPS

JULY 2

CEMETERY HILL

CULP'S HILL

JULY 3

PICKETT'S CHARGE

SEMINARY RIDGE

CLUMP OF TREES

CEMETERY RIDGE

PEACH ORCHARD

WHEAT FIELD

ROSE WOODS

JULY 2

EMMITSBURG ROAD

LITTLE ROUND TOP

DEVIL'S DEN

N

0   ½   1
SCALE   MILE

UNION
CONFEDERATE

west and north of Gettysburg, the Union army to the south. Neither side knew exactly where the other was.

On the last day of June, advanced Union cavalry elements in search of Lee's whereabouts reached the small town of Gettysburg, population 2,400. Just by chance, Confederate foragers approaching Gettysburg from the west engaged Union cavalrymen near the McPherson farm on July 1. Though neither Lee nor Meade had intended to fight at Gettysburg, this small skirmish steadily escalated into a full-scale battle—one of the greatest in American history.

Piecemeal, the various corps reached Gettysburg as fast as they could. Not until July 2 would the infantry elements of both armies be present on the field in their entirety. The effective strength of the Union army was ninety thousand; the Confederate army, seventy-five thousand.

Gettysburg was basically an infantry battle, with the units fighting in lines. The rifles used by both sides were muzzle loaders. It took roughly thirty seconds to load and fire each round.

The battle began on the morning of July 1, 1863, in the area of the Mc-Pherson farm west of town, with the Union First Corps holding the line. In the afternoon, the Union Eleventh Corps arrived, extending the Union line north of town. At the same time, Confederate forces were heavily reinforced. The Union troops were pushed back to Cemetery Hill, and the town of Gettysburg was captured by the Southerners.

On the morning of July 2, both armies established their positions as they awaited the arrival of remaining units. No fighting occurred in the morning or early afternoon. In the late afternoon the Confederates attacked the Union left flank at Little Round Top, Devil's Den, the Wheatfield, the Peach Orchard, and along the Emmitsburg Road. Union forces were defeated everywhere except at Little Round Top, where the Confederate advance was finally stopped. That same evening the Confederates attacked the Union right flank at Culp's Hill and Cemetery Hill, but the Union line held.

The Confederate efforts were renewed at Culp's Hill on the morning of July 3, but again failed. Having been thwarted in his attacks against both Union flanks, Lee gambled on a massive frontal assault against the Union center along Cemetery Ridge on the afternoon of the third. This action, known as Pickett's charge, ended in a Confederate disaster. A cavalry battle three miles east of town also resulted in defeat for the Confederates.

Both armies remained on the field on July 4, each waiting for the other to attack. No fighting occurred this day. Prior to dawn on the next morning, July 5, Lee began his retreat to Virginia. The battlefield remained in the possession of the Army of the Potomac from July 5 to July 7, as the various corps left one by one in pursuit of Lee. Not until shortly before dawn on July 7 did the last elements of the Army of the Potomac depart the Gettysburg area.

During the three days of fighting at Gettysburg, the Union and Confederate armies suffered a total of fifty-one thousand casualties, of which ten thousand were killed or died of wounds, thirty thousand wounded, and eleven thousand captured or reported missing.

The war continued for nearly two more years, but never again would Lee's army be able to take the offensive. In March 1864, General U. S. Grant was placed in command of the Union army. Basing his strategy on brute force and on economic attrition of the other side, Grant eventually pounded the South into submission. On April 9, 1865, Lee surrendered at Appomattox Court House, in Virginia.

From the perspective of hindsight, Gettysburg emerged as the turning point of the Civil War—the high tide of the Confederacy.

8

THE PRESENTATION

Because one of the basic purposes of this study was to inject a fresh breath of life into what has otherwise been an interesting, yet nonetheless disjointed collection of poorly researched illustrations, it was vitally important to present the photographs in a way that would effectively reveal their relationships to each other. Several possibilities were available: arrangement by photographer, by date of photograph, by chronological sequence of events as they occurred during the battle, or by geographic location on the field—the latter two options being the most appropriate.

Owing to the complex character of the battle, together with the fact that several important areas on the field were not covered by any of the early cameramen, the chronological arrangement was rejected.

Consequently, my choice was to present the Gettysburg series in the form of a photographic journey *across the battlefield* as it had appeared to the soldiers of both sides who struggled there during the summer of 1863. Though such a continuous journey at times breaks with the battle's sequence of events, a semblance of chronology has been maintained by commencing the tour near the point of the battle's origin and working southward.

To provide a framework for this presentation, the battlefield was divided

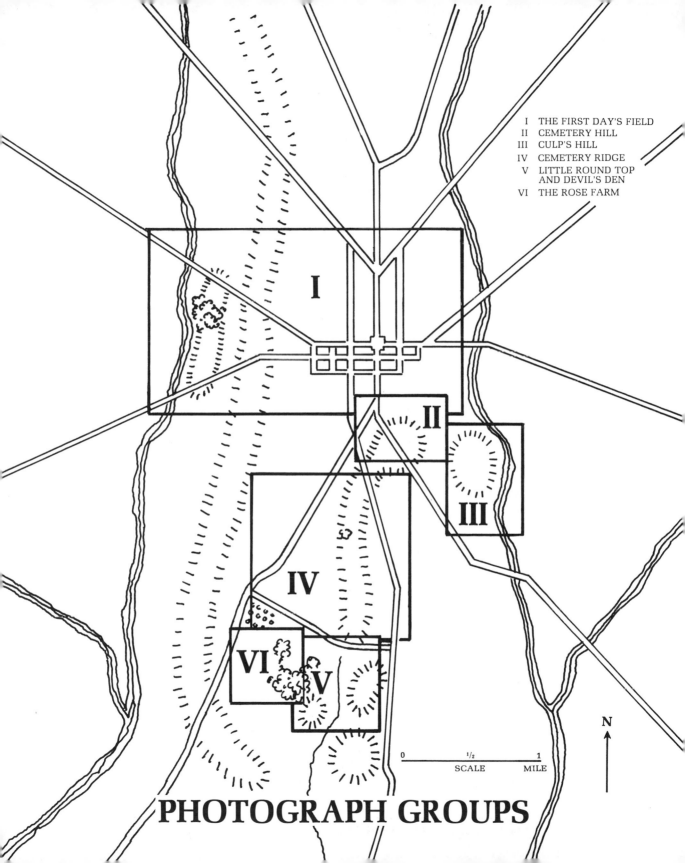

I THE FIRST DAY'S FIELD
II CEMETERY HILL
III CULP'S HILL
IV CEMETERY RIDGE
V LITTLE ROUND TOP
  AND DEVIL'S DEN
VI THE ROSE FARM

I

II

III

IV

VI

V

0   ½   1
   SCALE   MILE

N

PHOTOGRAPH GROUPS

into six areas: the first day's field (the north end of the battlefield); Cemetery Hill; Culp's Hill; Cemetery Ridge; Little Round Top and Devil's Den; and the Rose farm. Within these six geographic areas literally every known early photograph of the Gettysburg battlefield was made.

Three other items of the presentation deserve comment: the maps introducing each geographic group of photographs, the photograph captions, and the modern scenes that often accompany the original views.

The Maps

Each of the six groups of photographs has been prefaced by a map showing the position from which each scene in that area was recorded.

The purpose of the maps is multiple. Primarily they are intended to orient the viewer to the terrain, fixing in the viewer's mind the original location of the camera as well as the direction in which the camera was pointed. The maps also serve to relate each scene to the other photographs taken in the same area, thereby providing the viewer with a certain depth in his perception of that portion of the field. Modern battlefield avenues have been included to aid visitors in locating the scenes portrayed. All other features are represented as they were in 1863.

Wherever relevant, the maps also specify the location of individual military units, to help the viewer reconstruct the events that took place within the camera's field of vision. Only those units specifically mentioned in the captions are indicated, even though other units were frequently situated in the same general vicinity.

The Captions

Essentially the photograph captions are designed to provide the viewer with those items of information necessary for a full appreciation of each scene's historical background. The captions will be most informative when used in close conjunction with the respective area maps.

The captions consist of the title and the main text. Every title includes a brief description of the scene (these descriptions are my own—original titles, where mentioned, appear in quotes), the name of the cameraman or firm which took the view, the photograph's original form of publication (including stereo numbers, which do *not* reflect the order in which views were taken), the date or period in which the photograph was taken, and the source of the photograph reproduced in this book. (The sources are listed at the head of the index.) Because the photographers did not specify the dates on which they took their views, the dates in the captions, except for photographs of dedication ceremonies, must therefore be regarded as only probable. I use the symbol "o/a" to mean "on or about."

The main text varies from view to view, according to the material, but basically it places the photograph into direct perspective with the battle and with other Gettysburg photographs. Where significant problems were encountered while researching certain scenes, these are discussed.

The Modern Views

It is all too easy to view a historical photograph placed before us on the printed page as an object existing apart from reality. We may be vaguely conscious of the fact that each scene was indeed taken at some finite point, at a specific time long ago, but rarely do we feel the full impact of this knowledge just from the image itself.

Naturally the hands of time can never be reversed, and there is no way to literally transport oneself back to the moment of exposure. Yet the areas shown in the photographs in this book still exist. Somewhere on the twenty-five square miles of battlefield at Gettysburg lies the precise location of each and every view, and with research the majority of the camera positions have been precisely determined. That is the aim of the modern views—to show the scenes today of what was photographed over one hundred years ago.

By including modern photographs taken from the original camera positions, I have attempted to impart a feeling of time transcended and, in turn, to heighten the viewer's awareness that the moments captured by Gardner, Brady, and the other photographers were, and are, as real as the moments now being experienced in reading these very words.

Understandably, many of the scenes have changed their appearance in varying degrees. But owing to the almost continuous efforts of preservation agencies such as the National Park Service, permanent alterations on large portions of the field have been kept to a minimum. Aside from the natural expansion of the town of Gettysburg and the unfortunate spread of tourist-oriented commercial enterprises in the immediate vicinity of the town, the most notable change occurring on the field has been the growth of foliage, which in fact was great enough to preclude taking modern versions during the summer months. I took the majority of the modern views November 8—22, 1971, and the remaining ones during the winter of 1967–1968.

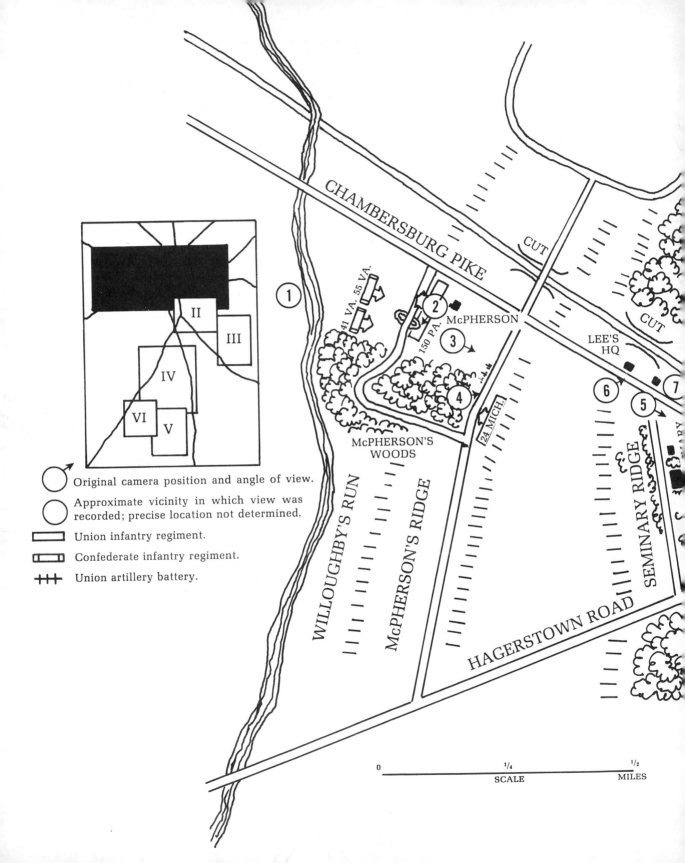

CHAMBERSBURG PIKE

CUT

CUT

LEE'S
HQ

McPHERSON

41 VA. 55 VA.

150 PA.

24 MICH.

McPHERSON'S
WOODS

WILLOUGHBY'S RUN

McPHERSON'S RIDGE

SEMINARY RIDGE

HAGERSTOWN ROAD

II

III

IV

VI

V

Original camera position and angle of view.

Approximate vicinity in which view was recorded; precise location not determined.

Union infantry regiment.

Confederate infantry regiment.

Union artillery battery.

0   ¼   ½
          SCALE   MILES

9

GROUP I: THE FIRST DAY'S FIELD

I–1 View along Willoughby's Run, Tyson, stereo #563, ca. 1865 (NPS).

It was in the area depicted here that the battle of Gettysburg began during the early morning hours of July 1, 1863. Commencing as a chance encounter between Confederate foragers and Union cavalry pickets, the fighting expanded rapidly as reinforcements from both sides were rushed to the field.

Although the original Tyson caption for this photograph did not specify where along the banks of Willoughby's Run the scene was recorded, the general lay of the terrain indicates that it was taken somewhere in close proximity to McPherson's Woods. The angular rock jutting into the stream in the foreground would naturally hold the key to the scene's exact location, if only that rock could be found today. Unfortunately, erosion and silt have changed the physical appearance of the stream's bank, and the rock has apparently been covered, either partially or fully, during the past century. The identity of the man standing on the rock is unknown.

Looking at the upper edge of the photograph, it will be seen that the negative number was scratched into the emulsion, or opposite side of the plate, and consequently appears backwards here. Such markings were usually cropped when the scenes were printed in their final form.

GETTYSBURG: A JOURNEY IN TIME

GROUP I: THE FIRST DAY'S FIELD

I–2   McPherson's Woods, view looking south, Brady, two plates, o/a July 15, 1863 (NA).

Intended as a single composite photograph, the two plates that made up this view were prominently featured as woodcuts in the August 22, 1863, issue of *Harper's Weekly*.

The first Union infantry reinforcements to reach the field in response to the cavalry's call for help were elements of Major General John F. Reynolds's First Corps. Though Reynolds was killed at the outset of the fighting, his spearhead unit, the Iron Brigade, stormed into McPherson's Woods from out of the left-hand portion of this view to shatter a Confederate force then advancing from the right. Victorious in this initial phase, the Iron Brigade was soon joined on its right flank (foreground) by a second unit, the Pennsylvania Bucktails, whose nickname derived from its mem-

bers' skill as marksmen. Each man proudly wore a bucktail on his cap. In a line stretching from the camera side of the pond toward McPherson's Woods, the 150th Pennsylvania Regiment of the Bucktail Brigade fought off successive Southern assaults during the afternoon's fighting.

But no amount of skill could stem indefinitely the relentless tide of ever-increasing enemy pressure. Finally, at approximately four o'clock in the afternoon, Northern positions on the McPherson farm began to crumble. Outnumbered and under direct pressure from two Virginia regiments (41st and 55th), the 150th Pennsylvania retired with the remainder of the Bucktail Brigade to a secondary line along Seminary Ridge.

Why Mathew Brady chose to entitle the scene "Wheatfield in which General Reynolds was shot" cannot be determined with certainty. The next picture, also by Brady, suggests his awareness that Reynolds actually fell

1–2

within the woodline and at a different location. Most likely, the title was chosen to capitalize on Reynolds's name. The significance of this discrepancy is discussed later (VI–13, 14).

Despite several obvious changes that have occurred over the years, McPherson's Woods, with its surrounding fields, appears today much as it did in 1863. The man posed beside the rail fence in the original view is none other than Brady himself.

I–2, Modern

GETTYSBURG: A JOURNEY IN TIME

I–3 The eastern edge of McPherson's Woods, view looking toward Seminary Ridge, Brady, plate, o/a July 15, 1863 (LC).

Falling back through these open fields, the Bucktails made their way as best they could toward the temporary shelter of Seminary Ridge. At one point during the retreat and probably in the cornfield seen here, the color-bearer of the 150th Pennsylvania, Sergeant Samuel Pfiffer of Company I, turned toward the pursuing Confederates and defiantly stood waving the American flag. For Sergeant Pfiffer, death came swiftly, but not before his actions were observed by Confederate Lieutenant General A. P. Hill, who noted with regret in his official report the death of that gallant enemy color-bearer.[25]

By the time the Bucktails and other retreating Northern units reached Seminary Ridge, a hastily constructed line of breastworks had already been prepared. The woodline along that ridge is clearly visible in the distant background of Brady's view. Also visible, rising above the trees, is the cupola of the Lutheran Seminary, used as a Union observatory during the first day's battle (9, 10).

Standing in the foreground of this view are Brady (right) and one of his assistants. Because the assistant is pointing toward the eastern edge of McPherson's Woods where Union General Reynolds was killed during the early hours of the battle, one can assume that Brady was familiar enough with the battle to know that Reynolds did not fall in the field depicted by the preceding view.

I–3, Modern

I–3

I–4

I–4 Scene of General Reynolds's death, Tyson, stereo #569, ca. 1865 (Darrah).

It was here, just inside the eastern edge of McPherson's Woods, at a point marked by the "R" (appears as a black mark on the thick oak), that the commander of the Union First Corps was killed. Anxious to personally position his units during the critical early stages of the battle, General Reynolds was directing the Iron Brigade into the woods when an enemy bullet pierced his skull. The highest ranking officer from either side to fall at Gettysburg, Reynolds, in death, would emerge as one of the greatest heroes of the war.

Today a monument replaces the oak at the point where Reynolds fell. Against the base of the original tree and probably placed there for effect by the Tysons, lies one of the thousands of temporary headboards which dotted the battlefield during the early days following the battle.

According to the weatherworn inscription, the soldier whose grave it once marked was a member of the 24th Michigan Regiment. Though difficult to decipher, the name appears to read "Williams," and may refer to W. Williams of Company B, 24th Michigan. During the winter of 1863–1864, Williams's body was transferred from the field to the Soldiers' National Cemetery in Gettysburg, where his grave may still be seen today (grave #5, Michigan section). The 24th Michigan of the famed Iron Brigade suffered a staggering 80 percent casualties at McPherson's Woods.

In the right background of the modern photograph are the guns and monument designating the position of Battery L, 1st New York Light Artillery. This battery provided support for both the Bucktails and the Iron Brigade on July 1 (see also view II-5).

I–4, Modern

I–5

I–5, Modern

I–5   Confederate prisoners on Seminary Ridge, Brady, stereo #2397, o/a July 15, 1863 (LC).

The above title specifies for the first time the precise location of this famous scene, one of the finest records of Confederate uniforms. The location was established by comparing the background with Brady's panoramic view of Gettysburg (7). Among the several distinguishing features present in both scenes is the mammoth tree standing unchallenged on the crest of the distant Cemetery Hill (on the horizon to the left of the first soldier).[26]

The fact that these three prisoners were photographed by Brady on Seminary Ridge approximately two weeks after the battle indicates that they may have been stragglers, captured during Union mop-up operations somewhere along either the Chambersburg Pike or Hagerstown Road, Lee's main routes of retreat. Certainly it was just by chance that the prisoners happened to be on Seminary Ridge when Brady was working in the same area; as the exposure was made, Union guards undoubtedly stood only feet away.

Quite conceivably this view was recorded on July 15, the same day Brady is believed to have photographed the nearby headquarters of General Lee. If this is correct, then the soldiers pictured here were very likely among the twenty-five hundred Confederate prisoners transferred the following day, July 16, from Gettysburg toward Washington and thence to prison camps throughout the North.

Today a stone wall occupies the ground where breastworks once stood. A marker (not visible here) describes the stone wall as having been erected on July 4, by Confederate General Rode's division. But if the interpretation offered here is correct, then it would seem that the original breastworks were made of logs and not stone.

Detail of I–7

I–6

I–6 The Thompson house, Lee's headquarters during the battle of Gettysburg, Brady, plate (?), July 15, 1863 (LC).

Barely reaching Gettysburg in time to witness the defeat of Union forces at the end of the first day's fighting, General Lee quickly established his headquarters for the remainder of the battle at the residence of the widow Mrs. Mary Thompson whose home, built in 1779, was one of the oldest in the Gettysburg area. Situated near the crest of Seminary Ridge and along the main western artery leading into town, a better location for directing the battle could not have been selected.

The Confederate commander held staff conferences and ate several meals at the stone house, although his personal tent was actually pitched on the opposite side of the Chambersburg Pike, near the position from which this photograph was recorded. Either through fear or respect, Lee was treated as an honored guest by Mrs. Thompson, who may be seen seated on a chair with one of Brady's assistants posed beside her, with Brady himself, partially camouflaged against the foliage, posed to her immediate front.

A second photograph of this scene, taken only minutes apart from the first, is today on display at the Lee's Headquarters Museum. The second photograph, originally issued as a stereo view (#2481), bears the handwritten date July 15, 1863, and thereby aids in establishing when Brady's series was recorded.

I–6 Modern

I–7

I–7   The town of Gettysburg, view from Seminary Ridge, Brady, two plates, o/a July 15, 1863 (NA).

The scene shown here is identical to the one that confronted the retreating Union soldiers as they reached the crest of Seminary Ridge. Their final defensive positions crushed, the Northern forces fell back through these open fields and backyards into the town of Gettysburg, and then southward to a predesignated rallying point on Cemetery Hill (see II-3). The mammoth tree on the summit of the latter hill can be seen towering above all others on the extreme right horizon.

Leading into town from the right foreground is the Chambersburg Pike, which served as the main artery of escape for the Union First Corps. By the late afternoon of July 1, the pike and adjoining fields were scattered with retiring infantry units, horsedrawn artillery churning up dust at full gallop, ammunition wagons, and mounted officers.

Typical of Brady's documentary photographs, this view is rich in crisp detail. At the extreme left one can see the distant tents of Camp Letterman, a general hospital probably still under construction at the time Brady's scene was recorded. To the immediate right of the tents, and considerably closer to the camera position, are the buildings of Pennsylvania College (12); below these an unfinished railroad bed leading into town. The brick house in the foreground was the residence of Miss Carrie Sheads (8); the white building across the Chambersburg Pike, the home of J. Grimes; and

directly above the Grimes home, looming in the distant background—Culp's Hill.

Not nearly as dramatic as the scenes of carnage recorded by Gardner and his assistants, this Brady panorama nevertheless reflects the unsettled atmosphere surrounding Gettysburg just two weeks after the fighting. Damaged fences, in particular, are everywhere. But more poignant is the mound of light-colored earth seen amid the young peach trees in the foreground. According to a contemporary burial map of the field, this grave contains the lone body of a soldier from the North.[27]

Over the past century the town and college have expanded westward to such an extent that most of the ground depicted here, including the original camera position, is currently either occupied or obliterated by latter-day buildings. Consequently, the modern view was taken from approximately where the footpath appears in the foreground of the original photograph.

I–7, Modern

I–8   The Sheads home, Tyson stereo #566, ca. 1865 (Darrah).

Situated along the Chambersburg Pike between Seminary Ridge and the town of Gettysburg, the Sheads residence, also the location of Carrie Sheads's school for girls, was soon engulfed by the shifting tide of battle. As defeated Union forces streamed back from their shattered positions along Seminary Ridge, this building became a shelter for those seeking refuge from the withering enemy fire.

Among the latter was Colonel Charles Wheelock of the 97th New York Volunteers. Stumbling into the home, the exhausted colonel immediately headed for the basement, closely pursued by a band of Confederates who followed him downstairs. At gunpoint, an enemy sergeant demanded that the colonel surrender his sword. The demand was obstinately refused. Just then, additional Northern prisoners were brought in, momentarily distracting the irate captor. Returning to the colonel minutes later, the sergeant repeated his demand, but Wheelock's sword was gone, surrendered, he maintained, to another. Later, after the battle, Wheelock, having been taken from the house, managed to escape and returned to the Sheads home to recover his treasured possession, which, during the confused moments in the basement, and at the suggestion of Carrie Sheads, had been safely hidden under the folds of Carrie's dress.

Another Union soldier captured at the Sheads residence was Private Asa S. Hardman of the 3rd Indiana Cavalry, who also later returned, but for a different reason. Hardman returned to marry Louisa Sheads, Carrie's sister.[28]

This Tyson photograph of the Sheads home was taken from across the Chambersburg Pike looking north. The telegraph poles along the roadside, one of which is seen here, are present in none of the 1863 views.

I–8

I–8, Modern

I–9

I–10

I–9 The Lutheran Seminary, view from the east, Tyson, stereo #574, ca. 1865 (Darrah).

I–10 The Lutheran Theological Seminary, view from the east, Brady, stereo #2393, o/a July 15, 1863 (LC).

Built in 1832, the main structure of the Lutheran Theological Seminary was, at the time of the battle, one of the most imposing architectural features on the entire field. During the fighting the building served first Union, then Confederate forces as both an observatory and a hospital. There is little doubt that General Lee, his headquarters situated nearby in the Thompson house (6), had occasion to personally survey enemy lines from the Seminary cupola.

When Brady's photograph (10) was recorded just two weeks after the battle, the Seminary was still functioning as a hospital. Several Tyson versions were made, the one reproduced here (9) being representative of the group.

The southward extension of Seminary Ridge, named after this Lutheran institution, was occupied by the Confederate forces and was used as a staging area for many of their assaults against Union positions on July 2 and 3. Since the Confederates took the offensive at Gettysburg, little or no fighting actually occurred on Seminary Ridge after it was incorporated into the Confederate line.

Still standing today, and partially hidden by foliage in the modern photograph, the original Seminary structure currently houses the Adams County Historical Society.

I–9, Modern

I–10, Modern

I–11

I–11 Gettysburg from Seminary Ridge, Tyson, two plates, August 1863 (NPS).

After capturing the heights from which this panorama was recorded, as well as the town itself, a portion of the Confederate battle line was extended through Gettysburg along the Hagerstown Road, seen leading into town from the right foreground. The boards and rails of the fences along that road were probably removed by Southern soldiers for use in their camp-fires during the three day occupation. Beyond the town and to the extreme left are the distant tents of Camp Letterman.

Like the area depicted in Brady's panorama from Seminary Ridge (7), the portion of the field seen here has greatly altered in appearance since the mid-1860s. The original camera position for the Tyson scene, however, is still accessible, though latter-day landscaping has reduced the height of the foreground. The road to the left in the early view no longer exists.

I–11, Modern

I–12 Pennsylvania College, Brady, plate, o/a July 15, 1863 (LC).

Prior to July 1863, Gettysburg was best known for its two institutions of higher learning, the Lutheran Theological Seminary (9, 10) and Pennsylvania College (Gettysburg College). At the time of the battle the college consisted of three buildings, all of which appear in the Brady photograph reproduced here (see also 7, another Brady view).

For the students of the college, the morning of July 1 commenced as usual with classes at Pennsylvania Hall (built in 1837), the building to the right. But as the noise of gunfire drifted back from the direction of Seminary Ridge, mounting curiosity became unbearable, and classes were soon dismissed.

Shortly after noontime on July 1, the Union Eleventh Corps arrived on the field in support of the embattled First Corps, then engaged west of town. Marching through the streets of Gettysburg at double time, the Eleventh Corps extended the Union line across the open ground just north of the college buildings, a position it would hold until forced to retire later that afternoon.

As was the case with the main building at the Seminary, Pennsylvania Hall served as both an observatory and a hospital, first for the Northern army and then for the Southerners. One of the soldiers treated here was a young Confederate named Lewis T. Powell, who was wounded and captured during the third day's battle. Not about to remain a prisoner, Powell procured a set of civilian clothes and subsequently escaped to the District of Columbia. In July 1865, Lewis Powell, alias Lewis Paine, was hung for his role in the Lincoln conspiracy.[29]

As is clear from the modern version of Brady's photograph, the appearance of this portion of the field has changed considerably over the past century. Of the three college buildings standing in 1863, two remain. The center structure in the original view is seen to the immediate left of the crane in the modern version, while the cupola of Pennsylvania Hall can faintly be distinguished rising above the buildings to the right.

I–12

I–12, Modern

I–13a

I–13a   The residence of John Burns, Brady, plate, o/a July 15, 1863 (LC).

I–13b   John Burns, Brady, stereo #2401, o/a July 15, 1863 (LC).

Throughout the morning of July 1, as the thunder of battle rolled across the fields and ridges west of town at least one of Gettysburg's citizens found it increasingly difficult to control his emotions. During a noontime lull, John Burns, then nearly seventy years old and a veteran of the War of 1812, finally decided that he could no longer stand idly by as the fate of his nation hung in the balance.

Grabbing his ancient flintlock and a handful of ammunition, the old warrior set out along the Chambersburg Pike toward the scene of the morning's fight. At the McPherson farm Burns reported for duty to the bewildered commander of the 150th Pennsylvania Regiment; and thus it was that the only civilian from the town of Gettysburg to participate in the battle fought alongside his young countrymen throughout the remainder of that afternoon, suffering three wounds but surviving to become one of the most famous heroes of the battle. Even Abraham Lincoln, during his visit to Gettysburg that following November, requested to meet the "Old Patriot." Together the two men attended services at the Presbyterian church in town. Burns's home, seen here, is no longer standing.

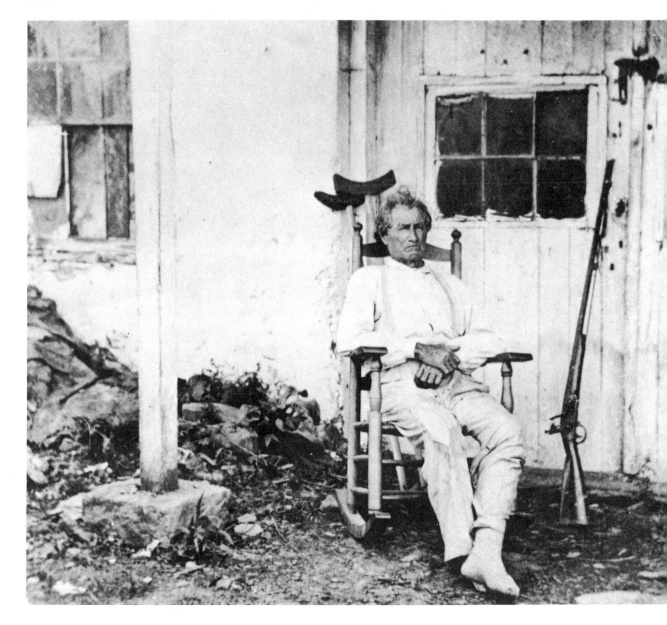

GROUP I: THE FIRST DAY'S FIELD

I–14

I–14, Modern

I–14 Chambersburg Street from the diamond, Tyson, plate, August 1863 (NPS).

For thousands of retreating Union soldiers, the town of Gettysburg, with its maze of unfamiliar streets and back alleys, became a living nightmare. In a desperate attempt to provide some sort of cover for the broken Northern forces, Captain Hubert Dilger, commander of Battery I, 1st Ohio Light Artillery, set up his guns on the town diamond at the position from which this view was taken. For as long as possible, Battery I fired round after round into the ranks of pursuing Confederates, then advancing on the town from the north along Carlisle Street, and from the west along Chambersburg Street. But the Confederate tide could not be stemmed, and finally at approximately four-thirty that afternoon, the 1st South Carolina Infantry, charging up Chambersburg Street past the buildings in this view, planted their tattered colors on the town diamond.

The first building to the left in the 1863 photograph housed both a savings institution and the clothing store of Gettysburg merchant George Arnold. The savings institution, today known as the Adams County National Bank, is still located on the same corner, though a more modern building replaces the earlier structure.

Several doors down Chambersburg Street was the Christ Lutheran Church (built in 1835), its steeple visible in both the original and modern versions. During the Union retreat through town, an unarmed Northern chaplain of the 90th Pennsylvania Infantry was shot down as he emerged from the church after caring for wounded soldiers inside. A monument now marks the step on which Chaplain Howell died.

I–15 Office of the United States Sanitary Commission, Gardner, stereo #238, July 7, 1863 (LC).

This view of the Fahnestock clothing store on the corner of Baltimore and Middle streets is the only scene known to have been taken by the Gardner crew in the town of Gettysburg.

Owned and operated by Mr. Samuel Fahnestock, the store, with its three stories, was one of the largest commercial structures in Gettysburg at the time of the battle. From its flat roof, Union General O. O. Howard, commander of the Eleventh Corps, upon reaching the town late on the morning of July 1, made his initial observations. It may have been here that Howard designated Cemetery Hill as a rallying point in the event Union forces were defeated that day. This choice became one of the most important decisions made at Gettysburg, for the establishment of a defensive position on Cemetery Hill enabled Northern forces to hold out long enough for the bulk of their army to reach the field.

The building became the office of the Sanitary Commission—the sign can be read above the door—on July 7. That day a strategic railroad bridge over Rock Creek, damaged earlier by Confederate forces, was finally repaired, allowing the direct entry of desperately needed supplies into town. The Sanitary Commission, a civilian organization comparable to today's Red Cross, abandoned its temporary headquarters at a school house south of town and relocated to the more centrally situated Fahnestock building.[30]

Thus Gardner's photograph of the Commission headquarters could not have been recorded prior to July 7. Furthermore, since most of Gardner's work at Gettysburg is believed to have been completed before sundown on July 6, and because he would not have lingered in Gettysburg longer than was absolutely necessary—he was eager to get his pictures on the market—the building was most probably photographed on the very day of the Commission's move.

Later that month the headquarters relocated once again—complete with supplies, ready-made sign boards, and personnel—to the general hospital at Camp Letterman.

The basic structure of the Fahnestock building is still standing. However, it has been greatly enlarged over the years and currently bears little resemblance to its 1863 appearance.

I–15

I–15, Modern

I–16   The German Reformed Church, Tyson, stereo #588, ca. 1865 (Darrah).

The German Reformed Church, situated on the corner of Stratton and High streets, was originally built in 1814 but was enlarged and rededicated the year before the battle. As were most Gettysburg structures of comparable size, the Reformed Church served as a temporary field hospital during the fighting.

Because of its location on a rise at the southeastern edge of town, the Reformed Church was an especially prominent landmark, clearly distinguishable from Union positions on Cemetery Hill, outside the town. To avoid attracting hostile fire, a red hospital flag was flown from the cupola.

One of the soldiers cared for at this church was Private Reuben F. Ruch, Company F, 153rd Pennsylvania Infantry of the Union Eleventh Corps. Ruch sarcastically commented in later years how, as a prisoner on the second day of the battle, he had witnessed, from one of the church windows, a nearby group of Confederate soldiers breaking open casks of whiskey just prior to their attack on Cemetery Hill (II-4).[31] The attack failed, but it was not for want of courage.

This photograph is an oddity among the Tyson battlefield views in that it was taken when the trees were bare. The Tysons were probably attempting to minimize the foliage which would have obscured the front of the building during the summer months.

I–16, Modern

I–16

I–17 The Adams County Prison, Tyson, stereo #564, ca. 1865 (Darrah).

Diagonally across High Street from the Reformed Church, and shown here in a view taken from the front yard of the Gettysburg Public School, stood the medieval-looking structure of the Adams County Prison.

On July 2, Alexander Skelly, a young boy who lived in Gettysburg at the time of its Confederate occupation, witnessed a sight he would never forget —the Confederate commander himself, General Robert E. Lee, mounted on horseback and accompanied by his staff, galloping up High Street from the direction of Baltimore Street. Lee's destination was the County Prison where a council of war was then being held.[32] In light of the prison's location at the southeastern edge of town, this conference was probably related to preparations for the Confederate assault on Cemetery Hill.

The original prison building currently houses the Gettysburg Public Library.

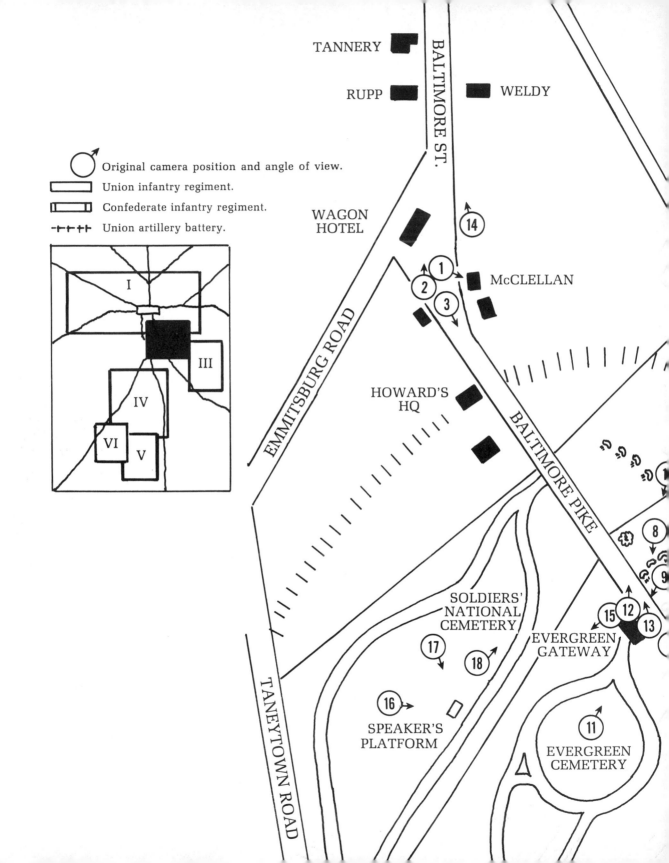

TANNERY

RUPP

WELDY

BALTIMORE ST.

○⟋ Original camera position and angle of view.

▭ Union infantry regiment.

▭ Confederate infantry regiment.

⊢⊢⊢⊢ Union artillery battery.

WAGON HOTEL

EMMITSBURG ROAD

I

III

IV

VI V

14

1

2

3

McCLELLAN

HOWARD'S HQ

BALTIMORE PIKE

8

9

SOLDIERS' NATIONAL CEMETERY

17

18

15 12

13

EVERGREEN GATEWAY

TANEYTOWN ROAD

16

SPEAKER'S PLATFORM

11

EVERGREEN CEMETERY

GROUP II
CEMETERY HILL

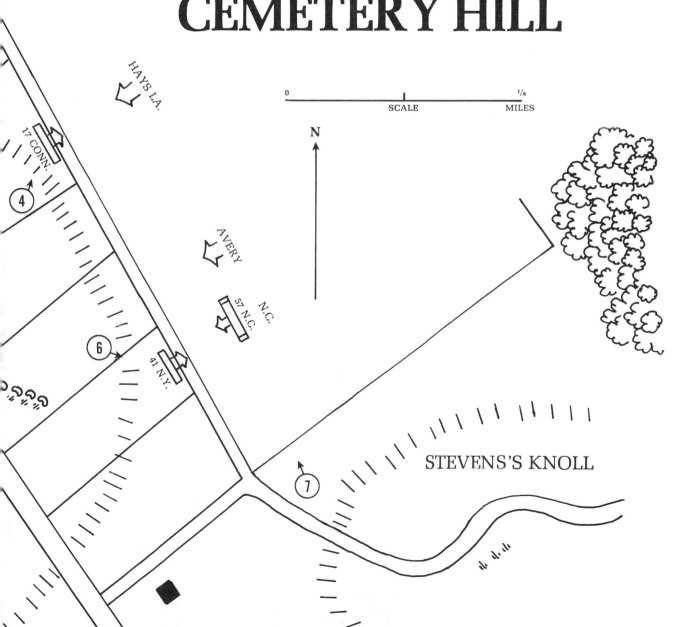

HAYS LA.

17 CONN.

4

AVERY

N.C.

57 N.C.

6

41 N.Y.

7

STEVENS'S KNOLL

N

0   ⅛
              SCALE   MILES

10

GROUP II: CEMETERY HILL

Leaving the scene of the first day's battle, we will now proceed southward through the town of Gettysburg to the scene of the second day's fighting on Cemetery Hill, and thence on to Culp's Hill. The reader should be reminded at this point that the sequence of our journey across the field does not strictly coincide with the battle's chronology. Hence, although Cemetery Hill and Culp's Hill are the next points to be visited, the fighting in the vicinity of Little Round Top, Devil's Den, and the Rose farm, while occurring on the same day, actually began several hours prior to the Confederate assaults against the two hills.

II–1 The McClellan home, scene of the death of Jennie Wade, Tyson, stereo #510, ca. 1865 (Tyson).

At the time of the Gettysburg battle Mrs. McClellan, whose home is the subject of this view, was still recovering from the birth of her three-day-old infant. Bravely remaining with her sister was twenty-year-old Jennie Wade. On the morning of July 3, Jennie was busy baking bread in the McClellan kitchen. Confederate sniper fire had been heavy that morning, but apparently Jennie felt secure behind the obviously sturdy brick walls. Then the unexpected happened. A Confederate bullet crashing into the kitchen *door* on the northern side of the house (left), and penetrating a second door inside, lodged in Jennie's back. She died instantly, the only civilian from the town to be killed in the battle.

Ironically, Jennie's fiancé, Corporal Johnston H. Skelly, of the 87th Pennsylvania Volunteers, was himself, at the moment of Jennie's death, lying desperately wounded in Virginia, a casualty of the battle of Winchester two weeks before. On July 12, 1863, Skelly succumbed to his wounds. Neither Jennie nor Johnston had received word of the other's fate.

While a portion of the fence appearing in this Tyson photograph is obviously in need of repair, there is no way of establishing whether the damage was the direct result of the battle nor, more significantly, the length of time the fence remained in its damaged state. The other Tyson stereo views recorded in the immediate vicinity were clearly taken at least a year or two after the fighting.

Today the original McClellan house is preserved as a privately owned museum, the bullet holes in the two doors near the kitchen still present. Jennie's grave, marked by a statue, is located in Evergreen Cemetery, just up the Baltimore Pike.

II–1

II–1, Modern

II–2

II–2   The Wagon Hotel, Tyson, stereo #511, ca. 1865 (Tyson).

Situated across Baltimore Street from the McClellan home, the Wagon Hotel afforded a commanding view of the southern portion of Gettysburg. After the town's capture on July 1, and throughout the remainder of the battle, the hotel served as an advanced outpost for Union sharpshooters who fought a persistent and lively duel with their Confederate counterparts stationed less than one hundred and fifty yards away in the home at the right, under the tannery smokestack (the residence of John Rupp, co-owner of the tannery.)

Before the war the Wagon Hotel primarily catered to teamsters who parked their wagons in the open lot adjoining the building (foreground). Sometime during the early years following the battle, the name of the establishment was changed to the Battlefield Hotel, presumably in an attempt to attract the newly born tourist trade. As is clear from the modern version, the hotel (see also 12) no longer stands and today a widened Baltimore Street replaces the lot in which wagons were once parked.

II–2, Modern

II–3 View along Baltimore Street, looking toward the crest of Cemetery Hill, Tyson, stereo #581, ca. 1865 (Darrah).

Approximately twenty-five hundred Northern soldiers were captured during the chaotic Union retreat through the streets of Gettysburg on the afternoon of July 1. For the majority of exhausted soldiers who managed to make their way successfully to the southern extremity of town, the scene that confronted them as they rounded the bend in Baltimore Street, shown here, must have invoked a feeling of deep relief. Awaiting them were four fresh Northern regiments supported by artillery, held in reserve on Cemetery Hill, under orders from General O. O. Howard. If Howard had not decided earlier that day to occupy the hill, a natural defensive position, the eventual outcome of the battle probably would not have been a Northern victory.

Appearing at the extreme left in this view, and barely part of it, is a portion of the giant tree which stood so prominently on the crest of the hill at the time of the battle. Diagonally across the road from the tree, and seen as a small dark mass on the horizon, is the gateway to Evergreen Cemetery, which we will examine in some detail in scenes 8, 9, and 10. Barely visible to the right of the gateway, looking like a candy-striped pole, is a portion of the entrance to the Soldiers' National Cemetery. Since the entranceway was not erected until roughly late 1864, the pole helps date the scene as circa 1865.

Dominating the right half of the view stands the three-story dwelling used by General Howard as his headquarters during the fighting on the second and third days of the battle. In 1866, the building was converted into a home for children orphaned by the war.

Today the area depicted by this photograph serves as a center for commercial enterprises catering to the battlefield tourist trade. Though the two buildings closest to the camera in the original Tyson scene are still standing, recent alterations performed when they were converted into museums have significantly changed their Civil War appearance.

II–3

II–3, Modern

II–4 Scene of the charge of the Louisiana Tigers, photographer unknown, two plates, July 1863 (LC, left; NA, right).

As the first day's fighting drew to a close, both armies settled down to the task of preparing for the next day's battle. The Union line was expanded and strengthened throughout the evening of July 1, and well into the following afternoon, with Cemetery Hill as its nucleus. By 4:00 P.M. on July 2, the new Union position, fully reinforced by the arrival of the five corps that had not participated in the first day's battle, stretched in an arc some three miles long from Culp's Hill (group III), to Cemetery Hill, and southward along Cemetery Ridge (group IV). Facing the Northerners along the entire length of this line was a victorious enemy, also fully reinforced and eager to repeat their performance of July 1.

It was at approximately sundown on the second day of the battle that the Confederate assault against Cemetery Hill commenced (along with an attack against Culp's Hill, examined in the next chapter). From hidden positions near the town emerged two brigades of Southern infantry, some thirty-five hundred men in all, commanded by Brigadier General H. S. Hays and Colonel I. E. Avery. Shown in this excellent panoramic view taken from the Union positions atop Cemetery Hill is the ground over which Hays's men—the Louisiana Tigers—advanced that evening, under the blazing rays of a setting sun.

At the outset, Hays's line extended from the German Reformed Church (center background, see also I-16), across the rolling fields to a point directly in front of the Culp farm (extreme right). Despite the murderous volume of artillery fire spewing from Union batteries (just behind the camera position), the Tigers pressed steadily onward, reached the base of Cemetery Hill, occupied at that point by several Union regiments, including the 17th Connecticut, and quickly broke through the Northern defensive line. Rushing wildly up the slopes, the Southerners lurched into the batteries. Hand-to-hand fighting developed and for a few tense moments, it appeared as if the position would be captured. Had the Southerners been reinforced at this critical juncture, the struggle for Cemetery Hill might have ended in a Confederate victory. But help did not arrive, and soon the Tigers were forced to retire under a staggering Union counterattack.

The two-plate panorama is one of the finest documentary scenes taken at Gettysburg. Its authorship is unfortunately unknown. That it was probably taken within a month following the battle is evident from the presence of the two soldiers seated in the foreground (to the right of the middle), the grazing horses, boxes of supplies, and campfire smoke coming from the extreme left (site of a Union militia encampment, see 12). Neither plate (one of which has been on occasion incorrectly identified as a view of Culpeper, Virginia) appears listed in Gardner's 1863 catalogue. Nor have I succeeded in locating either plate in its original form of publication. But the fact that it is an early two-plate panorama suggests, if no more, that it may have been taken under Brady's supervision.

A century later, much of the scene portrayed in the 1863 view is obscured by foliage. Clearly visible in the modern version, however, is the white shafted monument which today marks the position held by the 17th Connecticut at the foot of the hill during that bloody encounter on the evening of July 2.

II–4

II–4, Modern

II–5

II–6

GETTYSBURG: A JOURNEY IN TIME

II–5 View from the Baltimore Pike, looking toward Culp's Hill, photographer unknown, plate (?), July 1863 (NA).

II–6 View from Cemetery Hill, looking toward Culp's Hill, Tyson, plate, August 1863 (NPS).

The Louisiana Tigers were accompanied in their attack against Cemetery Hill by Colonel I. E. Avery's North Carolina brigade. Three regiments strong, the North Carolinians advanced to the immediate left of the Tigers against the position seen in the foreground of these photographs.

Approaching the thin Union line strung out along the stone wall at the base of the Hill, Colonel Avery's left flank regiment, the 57th North Carolina, suddenly found itself caught in a deadly crossfire from a hidden Union battery positioned on nearby Stevens's Knoll (see view 7).

The earlier of the two photographs reproduced here is the one that reveals the tent and the then recently constructed earthworks of Reynolds's Battery I, 1st New York Light Artillery (5). Although the view was taken within a month following the battle, its authorship is nevertheless uncertain. There is a possibility that it was recorded by F. Gutekunst of Philadelphia. One of the photographs listed in Gutekunst's advertisement of July 23, 1863, is identified as a view of the Union positions looking east from the cemetery. Yet, while Gutekunst's description fits the photograph accurately, there is currently no way of establishing whether this is the identical view referred to in the advertisement.

As far as photographic quality is concerned, the view recorded by the Tyson firm in August 1863 (6) is without question the better of the two. Produced from a point several yards down the northeastern slope of Cemetery Hill and looking toward neighboring Culp's Hill, this Tyson version affords a fine glimpse of the stone wall attacked on the evening of July 2. The portion of the wall visible here bordering the dirt path at the base of Cemetery Hill was defended by the 41st New York Regiment. Today a monument, seen in the modern photograph, marks the position occupied by that unit during its encounter with Avery's brigade.

II–5, Modern
II–6, Modern

II–7

GETTYSBURG: A JOURNEY IN TIME

II–7 Scene of the Confederate assault on Cemetery Hill, taken from below Stevens's Knoll, photographer unknown, plate, ca. July 1863 (NA).

The scene depicted in this photograph is similar to that which confronted Stevens's 5th Maine Battery (stationed on a grassy knoll hidden from Confederate view by the wooded slopes of Culp's Hill), as it patiently waited for Avery's men to pass across their direct field of fire. From right to left, over the rolling fields beyond the stone wall in the foreground, moved the Confederate line, steadily forward toward the enemy positions to their front. At precisely the right moment, Stevens's battery opened up on the Southern left flank, temporarily stunning Avery's line and shattering the 57th North Carolina Regiment.

But Avery's men were veterans and immediately after the initial shock, the Southerners pressed over the wall at the base of Cemetery Hill (visible through the trees to the extreme left), up toward the guns beyond.

As the rapidly darkening skies of late evening descended upon the field, Stevens's cannoneers continued to exact their toll, until finally the North Carolinians, unsupported and facing a Union counterattack from the direction of Evergreen Cemetery, could hold their ground no longer. With the retreat of Avery's brigade, followed closely by the retiring Louisiana Tigers, the struggle for Cemetery Hill ended in a Union victory.

That the view reproduced here was taken shortly after the battle is substantiated by the presence of the naked fence posts to the right, which are also visible in the Tyson view of these fields, recorded in August 1863, from Cemetery Hill (6).

Today the view from the base of Stevens's Knoll appears much as it did in 1863. One change which has occurred since the battle, however, is the addition of the stone wall which lies behind the row of brush dominating the foreground of the modern photograph. It is the second wall just beyond that stood so prominently in the 1863 view.

II–7, Modern

II–8   **The Gateway to Evergreen Cemetery, July 7, 1863, O'Sullivan, plate (LC).**

II–9   **The Evergreen Gateway, o/a July 15, 1863, Brady, stereo #2388 (LC).**

II–10   **The Evergreen Gateway, Tyson, cdv, ca. 1864 (Tyson).**

During the late eighteenth and early nineteenth centuries, the only cemeteries serving the citizens of Gettysburg were located in the various churchyards about the town. In 1853, after it had become apparent that Gettysburg's gradual expansion would soon require more spacious facilities, plans were developed for a new cemetery. The site selected was a scenic and peaceful hill on the southern edge of town, an elevation which, from that time forth (ca. 1854), would appropriately be known as Cemetery Hill.

Erected in 1855, the distinguished gateway to Evergreen Cemetery, isolated as it was on the very crest of Cemetery Hill, was quick to become a favorite subject for the battlefield photographers. The three major groups of cameramen to cover the field during the early days following the battle—Gardner, Brady, and the Tysons—each photographed only two features in common, Little Round Top (group V) and the Evergreen Gateway.

II–8

II–8, Modern

II–9, Modern

The earliest known photographic view of the entrance to Evergreen (8) was recorded by O'Sullivan at approximately eleven o'clock (based on the shadows) on the morning of July 7, just hours after the last units of the Army of the Potomac had departed the Gettysburg area. The recently vacated earthworks situated in the foreground, remnants of which may still be seen today, were occupied during the battle by the guns of Stewart's Battery B, 4th U.S. Artillery. Beyond the muddy foreground and seated in the wagon on the Baltimore Pike are some of the many civilians who flocked to the field shortly after the fighting to witness for themselves the scene of the momentous battle.

Posed in Brady's photograph of the gateway (9), taken approximately a week after O'Sullivan's, is one of two assistants who characteristically appears throughout Brady's Gettysburg series. Just inside the archway stands a militia guard, apparently aware he is being photographed. It is interesting to see that Brady chose not to include the earthworks in this scene, focusing instead only on the gateway.

II–10

II–10, Modern

When the Tyson brothers recorded their series of plates in August 1863, they produced a scene similar to Brady's. I have chosen to show here a Tyson *carte de visite* (10) taken, judging from the overgrown earthworks and the repaired fence, perhaps a year following the battle. Although the dark spots seen on the gateway windows may appear at first glance to be broken panes, they are in actuality reflections of the countryside to the north.

II–11 View in Evergreen Cemetery, looking toward the rear of the Gateway, Tyson, stereo #519, ca. 1865 (Darrah).

By 1855, the year the gateway was erected, the first burials in the newly established Evergreen Cemetery had already been made. As work on the grounds continued, bodies were removed from the local churchyards in which they originally had been buried, and thus by 1863, many of the inscriptions on the tombstones predated Evergreen's creation. A notable example was the grave of Gettysburg's founder, James Gettys, who died in 1815. The white shafted marker at Gettys's grave, one of the tallest monuments standing at the time of the battle, appears to the left of the gateway in the Tyson view shown here. The then young pine tree partially obscuring the shaft still stands more than a century later. Planted in accordance with the cemetery's name, the first of these evergreens was brought in soon after the cemetery's establishment.

Because of Cemetery Hill's tactical importance during the battle, Evergreen was fated to suffer heavily from Confederate artillery fire. Contemporary accounts of the cemetery's appearance shortly after the fighting tell of pock-marked and occasionally shattered tombstones with dead horses and broken gun carriages scattered about the grounds.

II–11

II–11, Modern

II–12 Gettysburg from Cemetery Hill, O'Sullivan, plate, July 7, 1863 (NA).

Atypical of the close-distance scenes characterizing Gardner's Gettysburg series is this sweeping view of the town taken from Cemetery Hill. With his camera positioned on the roof of the Evergreen Gateway, O'Sullivan has here captured Gettysburg as it struggled to recover from the traumatic shock of war.

Leading into the town from the foreground is the Baltimore Pike, partially obstructed by a stone wall which, during the battle, had been extended into the road by Union soldiers as a defensive barrier against a possible enemy attack from the direction of the town. Just beyond this wall, parked along the opposite side of the road, is one of two darkroom wagons used by Gardner's team on the field. Note the presence of the Wagon Hotel, situated near the bend in the road as it enters the southern extremity of town.

On the far side of Gettysburg looms the distant heights of the northern extension of Seminary Ridge (Oak Ridge), and in the town itself may be seen the spires of the Francis Xavier Roman Catholic Church and the Adams County Court House (right). Appearing beneath these spires is the camp of a Northern militia unit that arrived in Gettysburg on July 6, the day before this view was recorded.[33] With the departure of the last elements of the Army of the Potomac from the Gettysburg area before daylight on July 7, the task of guarding the town and its recently established government facilities was assumed by these militiamen, who remained in Gettysburg for approximately one month. A careful examination of Brady's panorama of the town (I-7), recorded from Seminary Ridge, reveals the identical militia encampment.

Due to the presence of a large pine tree which today completely obstructs the westward view afforded from the Evergreen Gateway, the modern photograph reproduced here was taken from the ground level.

II–12

II–12, Modern

II–13 Union gun emplacements on Cemetery Hill, photographer unknown, plate (?), July 1863 (Miller).

Incorrectly identified as the scene of Pickett's charge in Miller's classic *Photographic History of the Civil War* (1911), the actual location of this view was established by a comparison with the preceding photograph.[34] Both views contain the branches of the giant tree across the Baltimore Pike from Evergreen Cemetery, the nearby tents of the Northern militia encampment, and Stewart's gun emplacements in their foreground. Additionally, the tall tree that appears on the right horizon is identical to the tree in the left background of both views 4 and 18, which show adjoining areas.

I have not been able to uncover a copy of this photograph in its original form of publication, and while the scene was conceivably recorded by Gardner's team on the morning of July 7, it is not listed among the Gettysburg scenes in Gardner's 1863 catalogue. The likelihood clearly exists that the view may have been taken by some other firm, possibly Brady's.

II–13, Modern

II–13

II–14 a and b   Views looking north on Baltimore Street, photographer unknown, plates, November 19, 1863 (NPS).

Within a month following the battle, and under the initiative of the prominent local lawyer, David Wills, plans were set in motion to establish a suitable resting place for those Union soldiers who died at Gettysburg. The venture was to be a joint affair involving representatives from each of the seventeen Northern states which lost sons in the battle. The site selected for the Soldiers' National Cemetery was an open seventeen-acre plot on the summit of Cemetery Hill, west of and adjoining the local Evergreen Cemetery.

On October 27, 1863, the immense task of removing all Union dead from their hastily constructed graves scattered about the field commenced. The formal dedication—at which Lincoln would deliver his famed Gettysburg Address—was held on November 19, and by then several hundred bodies, largely unknown, had already been reburied.

At the junction of Baltimore Street and the Emmitsburg Road, an unknown cameraman patiently waited that day to record the procession of notables as they headed southward through town toward the site of the ceremonies. Perhaps fifteen or so minutes before the procession passed by the camera, the first scene shown here was taken (a), probably for the purpose of testing exposure time. In the more famous second photograph (b), the cameraman has captured the procession as it was turning onto the Emmitsburg Road from Baltimore Street. It is very likely that this exposure was made as Lincoln passed by, but as is clear, the view makes it impossible to distinguish specific individuals.

The prominent residence seen to the left was the home of John Rupp, who, with a relative, Henry Rupp, operated a tannery, located just beyond. The tannery's smokestack appears to the immediate right of the Rupp home (see also view 2).

The authorship of both scenes, as well as all other photographs taken on November 19, has not been definitely established. Although Alexander Gardner briefly mentioned attending the 1863 ceremonies in his *Sketch Book* (1866), not one view of the ceremonies may be found there. In fact, I have never seen a photograph of the ceremonies bearing a Gardner label.

The only substantial mention of a specific firm being at the event, as noted earlier, is a contemporary letter written by one of the Weavers of Hanover stating that he had covered the dedication ceremonies of 1863. On

the other hand, it would have been exceedingly odd had the Tyson brothers of Gettysburg not taken a number of views. Indeed, because the negatives for both scenes pictured here were found in the Tipton collection, the final repository of all surviving Tyson negatives, the chances are great that while several photographs of the actual ceremony (16, 17) may have been recorded by the Weavers, at least these two views of the procession could have been taken by the Tysons.

II–14a/b, Modern

Above left, II–14a
Below left, II–14b

II–15

GETTYSBURG: A JOURNEY IN TIME

II–15   The dedication ceremonies at the Soldiers' National Cemetery, view from the Baltimore Pike, photographer unknown, plate (?), November 19, 1863 (LC).

The first fresh graves at the National Cemetery appear in this photograph in the right background. The grave appearing at the lower right-hand corner probably contained the body of a Union soldier who was later removed to his state's respective section in the National Cemetery. Not until the following March (1864) would Samuel Weaver, the burial operation supervisor, report that his task had been completed. In all, some 3,512 bodies of Union soldiers were transferred to their final resting places on Cemetery Hill. But of this number, nearly one third would never be identified by name.

At the time of the battle, a sign stood near the entrance to the citizens' cemetery ironically proclaiming that any persons caught discharging firearms on the grounds would be prosecuted to the fullest extent of the law. Understandably the butt of many jokes, it is probably this same sign that appears in this 1863 photograph to the left of the footpath in the foreground.

Completely separate, the two cemeteries on Cemetery Hill are today divided by an iron fence, with Evergreen in the foreground.

II–15, Modern

II–16

II–17

II–16 Dedication ceremonies at the Soldiers' National Cemetery, photographer unknown, stereo #1160, November 19, 1863 (LC).

II–17 Dedication ceremonies, photographer unknown, plate (?), November 19, 1863 (NA).

These two views of the dedication ceremonies, together with the preceding photograph, were undoubtedly taken by the same photographer. Unfortunately his name remains a mystery. Perhaps they were part of the series claimed to have been produced by the Weavers. Regrettably, the odd negative number of the stereo reproduced here cannot be matched to any known number sequence.

But regardless of their origin, these views are among the rarest records in existence of the actual ceremonies at which Lincoln delivered the Gettysburg Address—a speech that lasted but two minutes.

The first photograph (16) clearly depicts the enormous size of the crowd gathered about the speaker's platform, visible as a rise to the immediate left of the distant tent. The gateway to adjoining Evergreen Cemetery (left background) and Culp's Hill (right background) also appear in this view.

The second photograph (17) was taken several yards north (left) of the first, looking toward the speaker's platform from a completely different angle. Note the change in relationship between the flagpole and the platform in each. This second photograph is believed to have been recorded during the actual moments of Lincoln's address, and according to a study conducted by Miss Josephine Cobb, the President's face may be distinguished among those on the distant platform.[35]

Today the site of the platform is occupied by the Soldiers' National Monument seen in both modern views. This monument, unveiled in 1869, was the first of hundreds to be erected on the field in honor of those who fell at Gettysburg.

II–16, Modern

II–17, Modern

II–18   View from the Soldiers' National Cemetery, looking northeast, probable Gardner, plate, July 4, 1865 (LC).

II–19   John Burns with officers of the 50th Pennsylvania Regiment, probable Gardner, plate, o/a July 4, 1865 (LC).

On July 4, 1865, two years after the battle of Gettysburg, and less than three months after Lee's surrender at Appomattox, a second dedication was held at the National Cemetery, the occasion being the laying of the cornerstone for the Soldiers' National Monument (seen in the modern views for 16 and 17). The only photographic firm definitely known to have covered the event was Alexander Gardner's.[36]

By this second anniversary, work at improving the cemetery was progressing well. One project still awaiting completion was the task of replacing all wooden headboards with permanent stone markers. Seen among the wooden markers in the foreground of view 18 are members of the 50th Pennsylvania Infantry. In the distance, across the Baltimore Pike, are the guns and men of Battery B, 2nd U.S. Artillery. Although both these units attended the 1865 ceremonies, only Battery B was present during the battle.

Disregarding the addition of the Soldiers' National Cemetery, this photograph provides an excellent glimpse of Cemetery Hill as it basically looked two years before. Since the position occupied here by Battery B was then occupied by other artillery units, one can readily visualize the scene's appearance on July 2, 1863.

Today, the entire background is completely hidden by foliage, purposely added over the years in landscaping the cemetery. The large monument to the left in the modern photograph was erected in 1893 by the State of New York, which, of all the Northern states, suffered the greatest loss of men.

Among the notable figures who attended the 1865 ceremonies was John Burns, aged hero of the first day's battle. Burns may be seen (19) seated, front left, with the officers of the 50th Pennsylvania Regiment at their Gettysburg campsite (unlocated).

II–18, Modern

Facing Page:

Top, II–18

Bottom, II–19

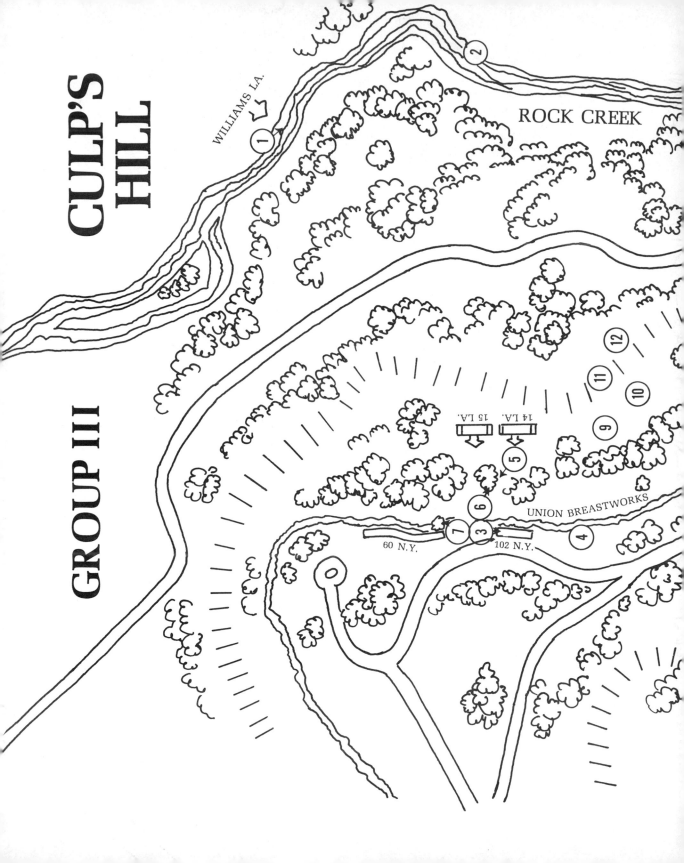

CULP'S HILL

GROUP III

ROCK CREEK

WILLIAMS LA.

UNION BREASTWORKS

60 N.Y.

102 N.Y.

15 LA.

14 LA.

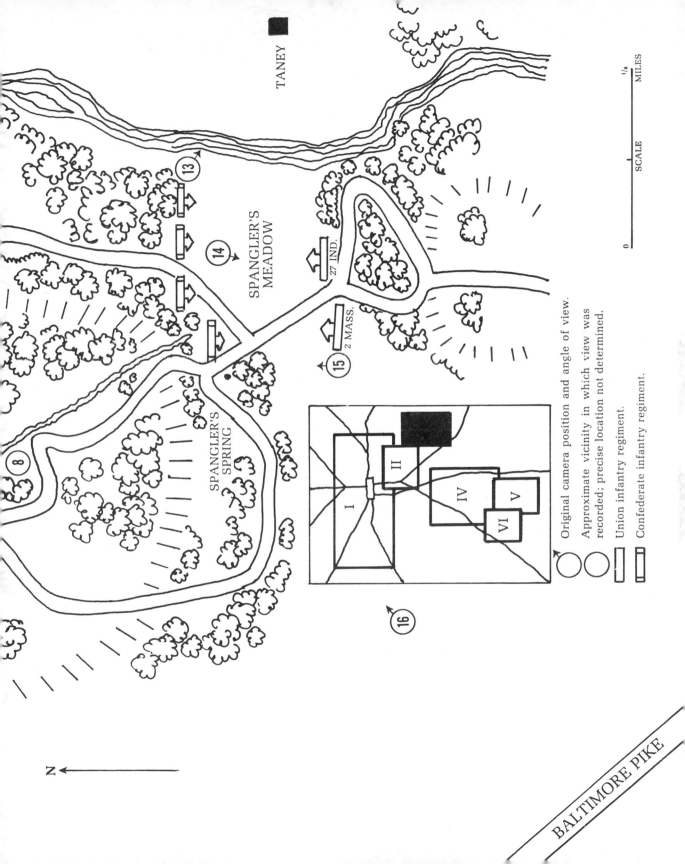

TANEY

⑬

SPANGLER'S
MEADOW

⑭

27 IND.

⑮ 2 MASS.

⑧

SPANGLER'S
SPRING

N ←

SCALE

MILES

0   SCALE   ⅛

I   II   IV   V   VI

⑯

Original camera position and angle of view.

Approximate vicinity in which view was
recorded; precise location not determined.

Union infantry regiment.

Confederate infantry regiment.

BALTIMORE PIKE

11

GROUP III: CULP'S HILL

III–1   View on Rock Creek where Williams's Louisiana brigade crossed, Tyson, stereo #502, ca. 1865 (NPS).

III–2   View on Rock Creek, Tyson, stereo #504, ca. 1865 (NPS).

In conjunction with their assault against Cemetery Hill, Confederate forces launched a simultaneous attack against the Union right flank, along the wooded crest of nearby Culp's Hill. At approximately half-past seven on the evening of July 2, under the cover of a rapidly darkening sky, three Confederate infantry brigades, commanded by Major General Edward Johnson, plunged across the waters of Rock Creek to commence their treacherous ascent up the hill's boulder-strewn eastern slope.

Union positions were not yet visible to the Confederates as they forded Rock Creek and entered the darkened woods on the opposite bank. But scores of bright yellow flashes from the rifles of Northern skirmishers alerted Johnson's men that stiff resistance would soon be encountered.

Shown here are two photographs recorded along the banks of Rock Creek where it flowed past the eastern base of Culp's Hill. Only the first view (1) can be located precisely. It shows the portion of Rock Creek that was forded by the Louisiana brigade of Colonel J. M. Williams, seventeen-hundred strong, who crossed in a column from left to right, re-forming their battle line on the right-hand bank.

III–3

III–3, Modern

III–4

III–3 Breastworks on Culp's Hill, occupied by the 102nd New York Regiment, Brady, stereo #2424, o/a July 15, 1863 (NA).

III–4 Union breastworks on Culp's Hill, Weaver, stereo #72,* ca. 1864 (Darrah).

Defending the eastern slope of Culp's Hill was Brigadier General George S. Greene's brigade of five New York regiments, spread thinly and badly outnumbered (due to the removal of the bulk of their corps, the Union Twelfth, to reinforce another portion of the field). Nevertheless, the men were deeply entrenched behind a line of fortifications constructed earlier that day. While these breastworks varied in appearance, depending on the tools each regiment had available, most were composed of felled trees and stones, reinforced with earth.

Brady's view (3), taken several yards directly up the slope from the boulder he photographed in 6, shows a line of both stones and timber. During the fighting on the evening of July 2, the breastworks at this point were occupied by the left flank of the 102nd New York Regiment whose battlefield monument appears at the extreme right in the modern version. A slight earthen mound today marks the original Union line. Interestingly enough, several of the trees surrounding the rock on which Brady's assistants were posed, gazing toward the enemy lines, are still standing.

The Weaver view of the breastworks (4), its precise location unknown, shows mostly timber construction. One of the Weavers, or possibly an assistant, is seen pointing toward the Southern positions.

---

* The number scratched into the left of the Weaver negative is greater than the number under which the scene was ultimately published. While the reason for this discrepancy is uncertain, it may indicate that more Weaver negatives were produced at Gettysburg than were subsequently issued. Early Weaver photographs are, in any case, relatively rare. As I have already noted, of the approximately eighty-five believed to comprise their initial stereo series, I have managed to locate only twenty-six.

III–5   The Confederate attack on Greene's line, Culp's Hill, oil painting by Edwin Forbes (LC).

III–6   Boulder used by Confederate marksmen on Culp's Hill, Brady, stereo #2386, o/a July 15, 1863 (NA).

III–7   Boulder on Greene's line, Culp's Hill, Tyson, stereo #536, ca. 1865 (NPS).

By eight o'clock in the evening, as the advanced line of Union skirmishers slowly retired up the dimly lit slopes back to the breastworks, Greene's New Yorkers anxiously braced themselves for the Southern onslaught now just moments away. The blue-clad skirmishers, firing their last scattered shots at the pursuing foe, suddenly dashed for the safety of the breastworks. With the Union front now clear of all friendly forces, Greene's entire line, some fourteen hundred rifles strong, erupted in a fusion of thunder and flame, piercing the darkened woods and ripping through the front ranks of Johnson's three brigades. The battle for Culp's Hill had begun.

Prominently situated in the area where Confederate Colonel Williams's right flank units, the 14th and 15th Louisiana, encountered the 60th and 102nd New York Regiments, stood two immense boulders some forty yards apart. Because both these boulders were soon to capture the imagination of the battlefield photographers, a fairly accurate painting of the vicinity, by noted Civil War artist Edwin Forbes of *Frank Leslie's Illustrated Newspaper* and based on one of his sketches drawn immediately after the battle, has been reproduced here. Seen in the foreground is the boulder that appears as the subject of Brady view 6, which was recorded from the opposite side with Brady's assistant looking in the direction of Rock Creek. As is clear

III–5

Above left, III–6
Above right, III–7

Far left, III–6, Modern
Left, III–7, Modern

from the painting, this boulder, together with smaller surrounding rocks, served as a shelter for Confederate marksmen during the fighting.

Pragmatically incorporated into the line of Union breastworks occupied by the right flank of the 60th New York Regiment was the second boulder—shown in a Tyson view (7)—which in the Forbes painting is up the hill and in the right background.

Though their images were undoubtedly etched into the memories of all who fought in that vicinity, these two boulders have long since ceased to attract the attention of latter-day tourists, who seldom venture far from the modern battlefield avenues. Obscured by foliage, the boulders today sit silently in the positions they have occupied for countless centuries, the scenes they witnessed that warm summer evening forever locked within.

III–8   View in the woods at Culp's Hill, Tyson, stereo #537, ca. 1865 (LC).

III–9   View in the woods at Culp's Hill, Tyson, stereo #523, ca. 1865 (NPS).

III–10 View in the woods at Culp's Hill, Tyson, stereo #533, ca. 1865 (NPS).

III–11 View in the woods at Culp's Hill, Weaver, stereo #71, ca. 1864 (Darrah).

None of the four Culp's Hill photographs shown here can be pinpointed; yet together they provide the modern viewer with an excellent glimpse of the hill's appearance only a year or two after the battle. Both the Tysons and the Weavers, fascinated by the grotesque quality of the trees—torn, shattered, and in some instances, actually felled by almost continuous rifle fire—devoted a considerable portion of their respective stereo series to this area. Brady recorded similar studies at Culp's Hill, but they were distinctly inferior to the later attempts of both the Tysons and the Weavers. Because bullets struck trees more than anything else, it is not surprising that much of the timber was either dead or dying from lead poisoning when photographed.

That the Tysons, in particular, were attracted to the artistic qualities of their subject matter is evidenced by the close-up view of the bullet-riddled trees in photograph 9. It is clear that this scene, as with many in their stereo series, was intended more as a nature study than as a general historic view.

Over the years the scars of battle have all been covered by the growth of those trees that managed to survive. Of the numerous original trees standing today, many still contain chunks of lead deep inside, embedded there during the battle.

Top left, III–8
Top right, III–9
Bottom left, III–10
Bottom right, III-11

GETTYSBURG: A JOURNEY IN TIME

GROUP III: CULP'S HILL

III-12

III-12   Confederate burial trench, Culp's Hill, Weaver, stereo #83, ca. 1864 (Darrah).

According to the original Weaver caption for this scene recorded at the eastern base of Culp's Hill, the mass grave in the foreground contains the bodies of "45 Rebels." Contemporary records reveal that 394 Southerners were buried on the eastern slope and at the base of Culp's Hill.[37] Because the site of this struggle was in Union hands at the termination of the fighting, most of these burials were performed on July 4 by exhausted Northerners who could not have cared less about preparing and identifying individual graves of fallen enemy soldiers.

Thus it was that the majority of Confederates were similarly interred in mass graves such as the one pictured here. These graves were viewed by visitors on the field for nearly a decade following the battle. While the last of the Northern dead were reinterred in the Soldiers' National Cemetery by the spring of 1864, it was not until the period 1870–1873 that the large portion of Southern graves were finally relocated. Under the initiative of a Southern women's organization, 3,320 Confederate bodies were transported during that period to cemeteries in Richmond, Charleston, Savannah, and Raleigh. Of this number, only a fraction would ever be identified by name or unit.

Of all the areas on the field at Gettysburg, Culp's Hill was among the earliest to be cleared of its dead, both Union and Confederate, during the initial burial operations. The task in this area was completed well before noon on July 5.[38] The exact position of the grave shown here has not been located.

III–13 View on Rock Creek, looking toward the Taney farm, Tyson, stereo #527, ca. 1865 (Darrah).

Situated on the eastern bank of Rock Creek as the stream emerged southward from the dense woods surrounding Culp's Hill, was the farm of Zachariah Taney.

By dawn on July 3, Taney's stone house, one of the only structures in the immediate vicinity of the Culp's Hill battleground, was located directly behind Confederate lines and undoubtedly served as a temporary field hospital for Southern forces during the day's fighting. (The original building has since been replaced by a dwelling that is no longer visible from the Tysons' camera position because of the growth of foliage along both banks of the creek.)

III–13

III–14 Spangler's Meadow, scene of the charge of the 27th Indiana and 2nd Massachusetts, Tyson, stereo #514, ca. 1866 (NPS).*

III–15 Spangler's Meadow, looking toward the Confederate lines, Tyson, stereo #515, ca. 1866 (NPS).

III–16 View looking toward Spangler's Meadow from the direction of the Baltimore Pike, Tyson, stereo #516, ca. 1866 (NPS).

Despite the fact that Greene's New Yorkers successfully held their main line against repeated Confederate assaults on the evening of July 2, the undefended breastworks just south of Greene's position, left vacant by the removal of their occupants to another portion of the field, were swiftly seized by the left flank units of Johnson's assaulting force. With the return of the bulk of the Union Twelfth Corps later that same night, the basic scenario for the next day's struggle was complete.

Beginning at approximately four o'clock in the morning of July 3, and continuing for almost seven hours, the Culp's Hill area once again reverberated with the roar of gunfire. As Southern forces renewed their pressure against Greene's line, now heavily reinforced, Union counterattacks were conducted in an effort to recapture the lost breastworks along the hill's southern extremity.

Of all the numerous unit encounters that took place that morning, perhaps none was quite as dramatic as the futile charge of the two regiments of Union Colonel Silas Colgrove's brigade across Spangler's Meadow, the subject of these three scenes.

Arriving back in the Culp's Hill area on the evening of July 2, Colgrove's men found themselves positioned on the wooded knoll seen in the left background of the first photograph reproduced here (14). The Northerners faced a strong Confederate line (no fewer than four regiments) then located in the woods directly behind the camera. As far as can be determined, Colgrove's order to initiate the advance was a tragic misunderstanding, for the open expanse at this point was clearly a death trap for any units attempting to

---

* My research on these three scenes indicates that they were taken later than most of the views in the Tyson stereo series, and possibly between 1866 and 1868. Due to their rarity, however, and since they indeed reveal Spangler's Meadow as it basically appeared to the soldiers who fought there on July 3, 1863, I have chosen to reproduce them here despite the fact that they may have been recorded up to two years after the closing date for this study.

136

III–14

III–14, Modern

cross. But reminiscent of the immortal charge of the Light Brigade, theirs was not to reason why. At approximately ten o'clock on the morning of July 3, the 2nd Massachusetts Infantry, accompanied by the 27th Indiana on their right, together some six hundred and fifty strong, began the fated attack across the open swale.

Halfway into Spangler's Meadow at a point designated by the small marker seen in the modern photograph, the 27th Indiana was forced to turn back under a galling enemy fire which had already claimed over a hundred

III-15

III-16

GETTYSBURG: A JOURNEY IN TIME

Indiana casualties in the space of a few brief moments. Courageously, the 2nd Massachusetts pressed onward.

It is clear from view 15 that the distance between the opposing forces was not great. Considering the tremendous volume of Confederate rifle fire encountered almost instantly, it is surprising that any portion of the Union line was able to reach those woods at all.

In spite of the overwhelming odds against them, the 2nd Massachusetts Regiment actually managed to secure and hold, for roughly ten minutes, the edge of the woods to the right of and including those appearing in the second Tyson photograph. Only when capture seemed imminent was the order to retire given. By the time the unit reached the safety of its former position, over 40 percent of its number had been either killed or wounded.

Spangler's Meadow at the point depicted in the second original view is today completely covered by small trees and dense underbrush, precluding a modern version. The rocks on the far side (middle), however, are easily found because they are situated only several feet south of the well-known landmark, Spangler's Spring, obscured by the trees at the right center. According to tradition, Union and Confederate soldiers together drank the refreshing waters of that spring during an alleged truce on the night of July 2. Unfortunately, this story, not supported by concrete evidence, is probably more legend than fact.

The final original view of Spangler's Meadow (16) was recorded looking northeast across the meadow and toward the Taney property (right center distance). The house itself (13) is hidden from view by the woods at the extreme right. It was from these latter woods and along a line running parallel to the rail fence traversing the center of the scene, that Colgrove's two regiments began their doomed assault against Confederate units at the base of Culp's Hill (left). Over the years, the field from which the view shown here was recorded has been left fallow and today is covered by dense foliage.

The futile charge of the 2nd Massachusetts and the 27th Indiana had no bearing on the eventual outcome of the struggle for Culp's Hill, and the fighting on the Union army's right flank ended in a Northern victory at approximately eleven o'clock on the morning of July 3. Perhaps the hill's greatest importance was its strategic location near the Baltimore Pike, a vital Union supply artery.

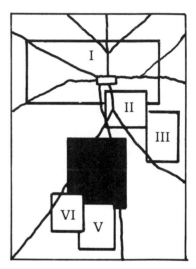

Original camera position and angle of view.

Approximate vicinity in which view was recorded; precise location not determined.

Union infantry regiment.

Confederate infantry regiment.

Union artillery battery.

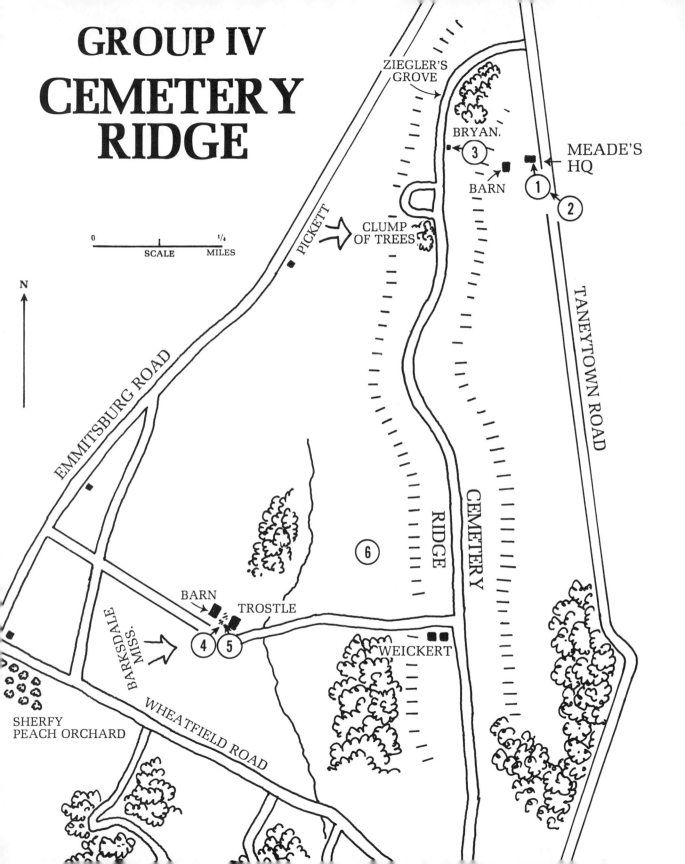

GROUP IV
CEMETERY RIDGE

ZIEGLER'S GROVE

BRYAN.

③

BARN

MEADE'S HQ

①

②

PICKETT

CLUMP OF TREES

0   ¼

SCALE   MILES

N

EMMITSBURG ROAD

TANEYTOWN ROAD

RIDGE

CEMETERY

⑥

BARN

TROSTLE

④ ⑤

WEICKERT

BARKSDALE MISS.

SHERFY PEACH ORCHARD

WHEATFIELD ROAD

12

GROUP IV: CEMETERY RIDGE

Having failed in his efforts to crush the Union right flank at Cemetery Hill and Culp's Hill, and the Union left flank at Little Round Top, Devil's Den, and the Rose farm on July 2, Lee decided on July 3 to launch a massive frontal assault against the Union center along Cemetery Ridge.

At about one o'clock in the afternoon of July 3, the Confederate artillery began an extended cannonade to soften up the Union positions on the Ridge. The barrage lasted two hours, but unbeknownst to Lee, most of the shells missed their mark and landed in the Union rear, in the vicinity of Meade's headquarters.

At approximately three o'clock, nearly eleven thousand Confederate infantrymen emerged from the woods on Seminary Ridge to begin their advance across almost one mile of open fields against the Northern positions along Cemetery Ridge. The encounter, since known as Pickett's charge (named after one of the Southern commanders involved, Major General George E. Pickett), was a complete disaster for the Confederates—only a fraction of their forces actually penetrated the Northern line and fewer than five thousand were able to make it back to the safety of Seminary

Ridge. The farthest point reached in the charge was a clump of trees—later to be immortalized as the "High Water Mark" of the Confederacy.

Both sides expected a resumption of the battle on the next day, but when further fighting failed to materialize on July 4, Lee decided to terminate the invasion and pull his forces back to Virginia. Pickett's charge, therefore, was the last of the numerous encounters at Gettysburg.

IV-1

IV–2

IV–1 Meade's headquarters, Gardner, stereo #259, July 6, 1863 (LC).

IV–2 The Leister farm, Meade's headquarters, Gardner group, stereo (number unknown), July 6, 1863 (LC).

Arriving at Gettysburg several hours prior to dawn on July 2, the Union commander, Major General George G. Meade, selected as his personal headquarters the centrally located farmhouse of Mrs. Lydia A. Leister, a widow, whose property bordered on the Taneytown Road just south of Cemetery Hill and at the eastern base of Cemetery Ridge.

Hidden from Confederate view by the gentle slopes to the west (left), Meade's headquarters nevertheless suffered heavily from Southern artillery fire on July 3 during the terrifying two-hour cannonade, forcing the Union commander to seek new quarters.

With the termination of the battle, a heartbroken Mrs. Leister returned to find her farm as it appeared in the two scenes reproduced here: strewn with festering dead horses and scattered with debris from the shell-torn buildings and fences. Seemingly unimpressed by the historic events that took place on her property, including a momentous council of war at which General Meade made the decision to hold his line at Gettysburg rather than withdraw, Mrs. Leister would for years complain bitterly of the havoc wrought upon her land.

The first photographs taken of the farm were recorded by Gardner on July 6. Though Meade was still on the field at the time, not departing until shortly before dawn on the following day, it is doubtful that he used the Leister home as his headquarters subsequent to July 3. At least three negatives of the Leister farm were produced by the Gardner team, two stereo views and an eight-by-ten-inch plate (which still awaits discovery).[39]

As is clear from the modern versions of the original photographs, both the Leister farmhouse and the barn have survived the past century. Today, they are maintained under the jurisdiction of the National Park Service. The huge circular Visitor Center seen looming in the background of the modern views was constructed in 1962 to serve as the Park headquarters.

IV–1, Modern   **IV–2, Modern**

IV–3 The Bryan house, on Cemetery Ridge, Brady, stereo #2396, o/a July 15, 1863 (LC).

Mathew Brady, like most of the early photographers to cover the battlefield, was anxious to secure several views of Meade's headquarters. But due to a misunderstanding, probably on the part of his guide, Brady unwittingly left Gettysburg with three similar views, including the stereo version shown here, of the wrong building. What Brady photographed, although he would continue to identify it for many years as Meade's headquarters, was the home of Abram Bryan, a free black, whose house was located on the crest of Cemetery Ridge less than three hundred yards from Meade's actual headquarters.

Brady's error, however, was a fortunate one for us. Rather than adding more views to the comparatively large collection of early scenes taken at Meade's headquarters by other cameramen, Brady's photographs provide the only views in existence depicting the Bryan house as it appeared in 1863. The house was completely remodeled several years after the battle, but based on the photographs, the National Park Service has since been able to restore the structure to its original condition.

IV–3

IV–3, Modern

Because Abram Bryan was a free black, it is understandable that he and his wife and two teenage sons, along with the majority of Gettysburg's black population, chose to flee the area when word of the Confederate invasion first reached southern Pennsylvania in June. Whether Gettysburg's black residents would have been returned to slavery if they were captured is uncertain, but Bryan at least was not about to take that chance.

During the battle, Bryan's home served as the headquarters of Brigadier General Alexander Hays, commander of the Third Division of the Union Second Corps. Hays's troops helped repulse Pickett's charge from this point on the afternoon of July 3.

While a portion of Seminary Ridge, the position from which the Confederate assault commenced, may be seen in the distant right background of Brady's photograph, it is regrettable that the noted photographer did not turn his camera ninety degrees to the left. Had a scene been recorded from that angle, it would have been the only known early view to show clearly, only two hundred and fifty yards away, the famous clump of trees reached by Pickett's men—a clump that was eventually to become known as the "High Water Mark" of the Confederacy.

Why none of the early cameramen chose to photograph the scene of the battle's climax is not altogether evident. Perhaps neither Brady nor Gardner was aware of the tremendous significance Pickett's charge would ultimately have. Granted, Brady recorded a distant view of the Union positions along Cemetery Ridge from Little Round Top (V-2), but that scene was intended as a general study of the field and not specifically as a view of the scene of Pickett's charge. As for Gardner, since the dead on Cemetery Ridge had already been buried by the time he arrived at Meade's headquarters, the vast expanse of open ground to the west apparently did not strike him as being a good subject in its own right—if he considered taking such a view at all.

But why the Tysons, who photographed the field for several years following the battle, did not cover that area remains a mystery. Not one Tyson image taken specifically of the scene of Pickett's charge may be found in either the 1863 series or among the numerous titles in the later stereo series. Not until the first monuments began sprouting up on Cemetery Ridge some twenty years after the battle would any notable interest be generated in photographing the scene of the charge.[40]

IV–4

IV–5

IV–4   The Trostle house, O'Sullivan, plate, July 6, 1863 (LC).

IV–5   The Trostle barn, O'Sullivan, stereo #266, July 6, 1863 (LC).

Considerably larger than either the Bryan or the Leister farm, but more typical of those that dotted the countryside surrounding Gettysburg, was the farm of Abraham Trostle, situated a mile and a half south of town. It was not for this reason, however, that the buildings shown here were singled out to be recorded. Gardner's was the only group of early photographers to cover the Trostle farm, and there is little question that the prime motivation was that it provided an excellent backdrop for the numerous dead artillery horses cluttered about the grounds. As is obvious in both views— one of the house and one of the barn—O'Sullivan had positioned his camera to give prominent display to the identical horses in each.

On July 2, during the struggle for the Union left flank, a Northern battery, Captain John Bigelow's 9th Massachusetts, was ordered to hold its position at the Trostle farm, whatever the cost.

Facing the battery, and advancing through the battle smoke across the open field behind O'Sullivan's camera position, was Brigadier General William Barksdale's Mississippi brigade, which had just penetrated the Union lines along the Emmitsburg Road. Bigelow's cannoneers, working at a feverish pace to stem the flood of enemy infantry, stood their ground, firing volley after volley into the rapidly approaching Southern ranks.

After a desperate hand-to-hand encounter the 9th Massachusetts retired, many of its number killed or wounded, four of its six field pieces captured, and fifty horses killed. But the battery's sacrificial stand had served its purpose, allowing Union forces enough time to establish a secondary position several hundred yards beyond the Trostle house (4, left background).

Today the house is slightly larger than it was in July 1863, but many original details on the farm, such as the artillery shell hole just under the diamonds on the barn, have been preserved. Seen on the rock in the foreground of both modern photographs is the monument erected by the survivors of the 9th Massachusetts Battery to mark the site of their stand.

IV–4, Modern
IV–5, Modern

IV–6   Dead artillery horse, Gardner, stereo #226, July 6, 1863 (Miller).

As with many of the views in Gardner's Gettysburg series, the specific location of this scene cannot be found in its original caption, which simply read "Unfit for Service." On the other hand, because Gardner focused most of his attention on photographing scenes with dead horses only after leaving Little Round Top but before reaching Cemetery Hill—he crossed the battlefield, it will be recalled, from south to north without regard to the battle's chronology—the chances are that this view was recorded somewhere near the Trostle farm (4, 5) or between that farm and Meade's headquarters (1, 2). The general character of the terrain supports that contention.

Since more than fifteen hundred artillery horses were killed during the battle, many of them shot deliberately by enemy units attempting to cripple an opposing battery's mobility, sights such as this, accompanied by the nauseous odors of decaying flesh, were common to early visitors on the field.

Though the task of burying the human dead was completed by the Army of the Potomac prior to its departure from Gettysburg, hundreds of horse carcasses were left uncovered. The immense chore of eliminating this health hazard was assumed by the militia. Taking advantage of their additional responsibility of guarding the battlefield against civilian removal of government property, the militiamen devised an ingenious scheme for soliciting "volunteers" to aid in their disagreeable task: civilians caught carrying off government property were given the choice of either being arrested, or of spending a certain amount of time burying dead horses.

IV–6

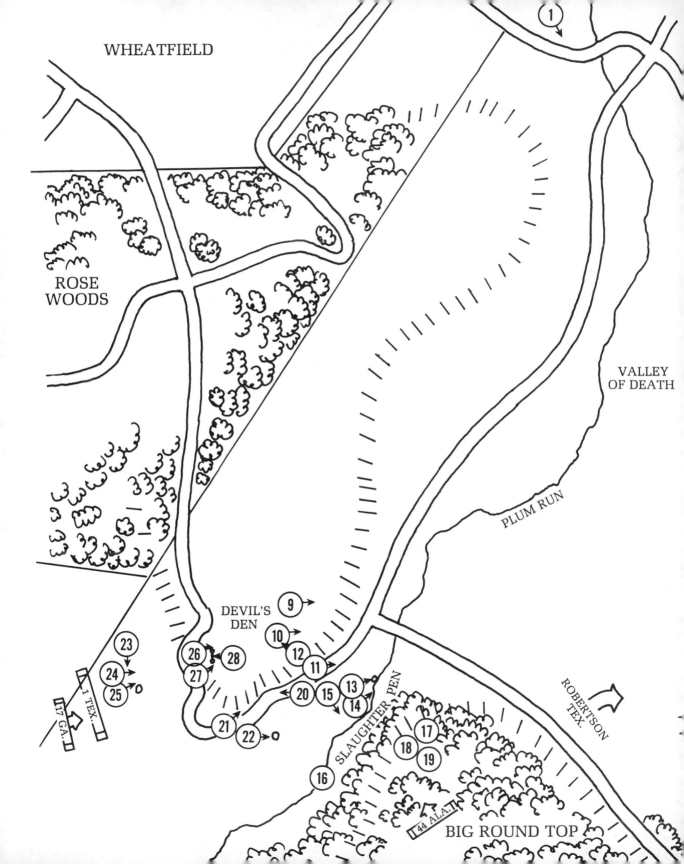

GROUP V
LITTLE ROUND TOP
AND
DEVIL'S DEN

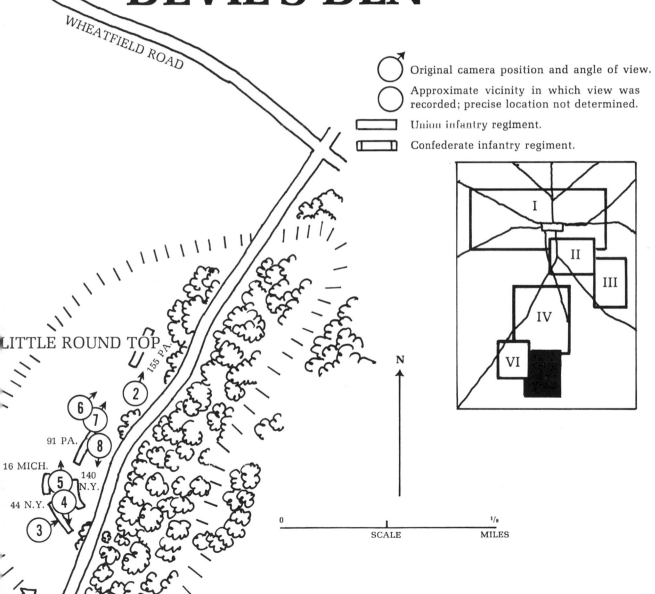

WHEATFIELD ROAD

⊙ Original camera position and angle of view.

◯ Approximate vicinity in which view was recorded; precise location not determined.

▭ Union infantry regiment.

▭ Confederate infantry regiment.

LITTLE ROUND TOP

155 PA.

②

⑥ ⑦

91 PA.

⑧

16 MICH.

⑤ 140 N.Y.

44 N.Y. ④

③

LAW ALA.

I

II

III

IV

VI

N

0 ⅛

SCALE MILES

13

GROUP V: LITTLE ROUND TOP AND DEVIL'S DEN

V–1 Little Round Top and Big Round Top, view from the northwest, Brady, plate, o/a July 15, 1863 (LC).

According to Meade's plan of battle for the second day, the Union left flank was to be occupied by Major General Daniel E. Sickles's Third Corps, which was to extend directly southward from the Second Corps positions on Cemetery Ridge. But Meade's orders were decidedly vague. Thus early in the afternoon of July 2, General Sickles took it upon himself to advance the entire Third Corps westward, forming a salient running from Devil's Den to the Peach Orchard and northward along the Emmitsburg Road, leaving Little Round Top, for all practical purposes, completely undefended.

Little Round Top, with its western face cleared by chance the year before the battle, afforded the finest panoramic view then available of the countryside south of Gettysburg (2). Yet, oddly enough, the hill's tactical importance was first seriously recognized by the Northern high command only moments prior to the Confederate assault against that point on July 2.

Reaching the hill during the final re-analysis of the Union positions, Meade's chief engineer, Brigadier General G. K. Warren, was aghast to discover Little Round Top unoccupied by anyone save a small detachment of signalmen. With binoculars in hand, the general quickly surveyed the distant woods to the west for signs of an impending enemy attack. To his dismay, all the signs were present. Frantic, Warren immediately dispatched messengers to seek aid.

As luck had it, a Union brigade of the Fifth Corps was at that moment marching along the Wheatfield Road past the hill on the way to reinforce Sickles's line. Hearing from Warren, the brigade commander, Colonel Strong Vincent, disregarded all previous orders and, without awaiting direct word from his own division commander, instantly diverted his four regiments back toward the hill, arriving a mere ten minutes before the Confederates.

Recorded from a camera position adjoining the Wheatfield Road, Brady's photograph shows both Little Round Top (left) and Big Round Top (right) only two weeks after the battle. Brady himself may be seen to the far left, gazing across the marshy flatland since known as the Valley of Death.

V–1

V–1, Modern

V–2

GETTYSBURG: A JOURNEY IN TIME

V–2 Scene looking northward toward Cemetery Hill from the crest of Little Round Top, Brady, stereo #2384, o/a July 15, 1863 (LC).

Precisely how vital Little Round Top was to the defense of the Union lines at Gettysburg is clearly revealed by this terrain study, the only early photograph to provide a general view of the ground between Little Round Top and Cemetery Hill. (A portion of the background seen here also appears in Brady view 7.)

While it is unfortunate that Brady did not record a large eight-by-ten-inch version of this scene, it is perhaps more regrettable that he chose to emphasize the large boulder in the foreground, thus partially obstructing the distant panorama.

Many important landmarks, however, are visible, including the Wheatfield Road at the northern base of Little Round Top (traversing the ground seen between the boulder and the large tree to the right); the farm of George Weikert (to the immediate right and on level with the top of the boulder); Ziegler's Grove (left center horizon); and some woods behind Evergreen Cemetery (right center horizon). Though difficult to discern, the famous clump of trees reached by Pickett's men during their charge also appears on the horizon line to the left of Ziegler's Grove. (There is a triangle formed by the three small groups of trees directly upward from the white rock in the foreground—the famous clump is at the top of this triangle.)

Today much of the open ground visible in the distance is covered by woods. Because a small tree has grown on the site of Brady's camera position, the modern version has been recorded approximately one yard down from the original location. Barely seen in the modern photograph are the monument marking the line of the 155th Pennsylvania Regiment (left), soon to join in the struggle for the hill, and the white rotunda of the National Park Visitor Center at distant Ziegler's Grove.

V–2, Modern

V–3

V–3, Modern

V–3 Union breastworks on the southern slope of Little Round Top, Gibson, stereo #261, July 6, 1863 (LC).

V–4 Union breastworks on the southern crest of Little Round Top, Gardner, stereo #247,* July 6, 1863 (LC).

V–5 Union breastworks on the southern crest of Little Round Top, O'Sullivan, stereo #230, July 6, 1863 (LC).

Being the first Northerners to reach Little Round Top in response to the desperate call for help, Colonel Vincent's brigade hastily took positions on the southern slope several yards from the summit, and prepared to meet the enemy then advancing through the timber on Big Round Top.

At approximately 4:30 P.M., the Union line was struck head on by four Alabama regiments under the command of Brigadier General Evander M. Law, who was soon reinforced by two Texas regiments of Brigadier General Jerome B. Robertson's brigade. Outnumbered, Vincent's men struggled to hold their line against repeated Southern assaults. But the situation grew steadily worse as additional enemy units, unleashed by the eventual Confederate capture of Devil's Den, stormed up the rocky slopes against Vincent's right flank regiments, the 44th New York and the 16th Michigan.

Suddenly, just as the Michigan regiment began to dissolve and all hope seemed lost, help arrived. Sweeping over the crest of the hill and plunging straight into the advancing enemy ranks was Colonel Patrick O'Rorke's 140th New York Volunteers, part of a brigade commanded by Brigadier General Stephen H. Weed. The Confederate units reeled down the slope, their attack stalled long enough for a battery of Union artillery and the remainder of Weed's brigade (including the 91st and 155th Pennsylvania regiments) to reach the summit of the hill. Among those who would not live to enjoy the fruits of victory, however, were Vincent, O'Rorke, and Weed. All three were killed or mortally wounded before the day's fighting had ended.

Shortly after sundown on July 2, Northern forces, anticipating a renewal of Confederate efforts, set about strengthening their defensive line by constructing a network of parallel stone walls. Reproduced here are three photographs of those Union positions.

Visible in the first scene (3), recorded slightly down the slope and looking

* Although the original negative is marked #248, this view was issued as #247.

back toward the crest as the Southerners would have viewed it, are the breastworks of both the 44th (foreground) and 140th (background) New York regiments. The next two views (4, 5), which look in opposite directions but were taken only several feet apart, show sections of the latter wall. The pine tree in the last photograph still stands today.

V–4

V–4, Modern

V–5

V–5, Modern

V–6   Union breastworks on Little Round Top, view looking north, Gibson, stereo #231, July 6, 1863 (LC).

V–7   Union breastworks on Little Round Top, view looking north, Brady, stereo #2387, o/a July 15, 1863 (LC).

Reproduced here are two similar photographs, one by Gibson and the other by Brady. They were taken only several feet apart, a matter of pure coincidence, since neither photographer was aware of the other's work at the time. This striking coincidence offers an excellent opportunity to compare the circumstances that confronted the two groups of cameramen. Gibson, forced to contend with frequently changing and often difficult

V–6

atmospheric conditions, was unable to achieve the clarity of detail evident in Brady's view, especially in the distant background. (Gardner's assistants at Gettysburg were all competent professionals, so the possibility is distinctly remote that the poor quality of Gibson's scene was due to sloppy workmanship.)

While the stone wall visible here has been preserved over the intervening years, dense underbrush currently covers the western slopes of Little Round Top, prohibiting the taking of a modern version. However, the spot is easily found today, for it is located just a few yards from the statue of General Warren, which now stands atop the boulder appearing in Brady's scene directly above the rail leaning against the pine tree (right).

V–7

2387

V–8

GETTYSBURG: A JOURNEY IN TIME

V–8   View from the summit of Little Round Top, looking south toward Big Round Top, Brady, stereo #2399, o/a July 15, 1863 (LC).

The stone walls constructed on Little Round Top after the heavy fighting of July 2 proved their worth the following day by providing Union forces with shelter against the harassing fire of enemy snipers lodged in Devil's Den—a group of enormous boulders located opposite the Round Tops and captured by the Confederates on the afternoon of the second.

The imagination can readily picture scores of Northern soldiers huddled against these walls on July 3, as scattered rounds from Confederate sharpshooters whizzed overhead. But considering the many long hours eventually spent behind the walls, life for these veterans must have gone on as usual, with idle conversation, a chaw of tobacco, and an occasional cup of coffee serving as relief from the anxieties of waiting for a renewed enemy assault —which would never come.

The same assistant seen in so many of Brady's Gettysburg views is posed here by the breastworks, seated facing Devil's Den. The original stone wall, occupied at this point by the 91st Pennsylvania Regiment, has since been replaced by a modern wall as part of a paved exhibit platform constructed by the National Park Service.

V–8, Modern

165

V–9   Little Round Top from the west, O'Sullivan, plate, July 6, 1863 (LC).

V–10   Little Round Top, view from Devil's Den, Gibson, stereo #267, July 6, 1863 (LC).

V–11   Little Round Top from Devil's Den, O'Sullivan, two plates, July 6, 1863 (LC).

An imposing sight by any standards, Little Round Top was doubly so for thousands of Southern infantrymen who strove to scale the rocky western slope.

In the first scene (9), recorded by O'Sullivan from the ridgeline just north of Devil's Den, several important features may be distinguished: Plum Run

V–9

V–9, Modern

(later known as Bloody Run) barely visible in the foreground flowing through the Valley of Death; and the breastworks of Vincent's Union brigade (3, 4, 5), on the upper slopes of Little Round Top to the far right.

Gibson's stereo version (10), taken from atop an immense boulder in the Den, was less successful in terms of quality than O'Sullivan's but equally interesting as an image in its failure—for just as the mists have here obscured the crest of Little Round Top, so too was the hill clouded during the

V–10

V–10, Modern

V–11

V–11, Modern

GETTYSBURG: A JOURNEY IN TIME

actual fighting by smoke from countless volleys of Northern artillery and infantry fire. (Why Gibson chose not to wait for the mist to clear, as did O'Sullivan, can only be surmised.)

The third scene (11) was taken by O'Sullivan directly below the boulder from which Gibson's view was recorded. The two trees appearing in the center foreground of Gibson's photograph are identical to those seen in the center foreground of this view.

O'Sullivan's photograph is unique in one respect. It is the only documented attempt by a member of Gardner's crew at Gettysburg to deliberately record a composite panorama. Taken just before Gardner's cameramen proceeded on to Little Round Top, and just after the bulk of Gardner's Gettysburg series had been completed—the views of the dead—O'Sullivan probably decided at this point to be more extravagant in his use of negative plates. Possibly he presumed that not much of great interest lay ahead since the last of the bodies, the group's main objective at Gettysburg, were then being rapidly buried.

Over the years, the most notable change that has occurred in the westward view from Devil's Den, disregarding of course the modern battlefield avenues, has been the growth of the woods at the base of Big Round Top, which currently extends into, and blocks out the right-hand portions of two of the views seen here (10, 11). Fortunately changes such as these (which, as we shall see, can sometimes hinder an accurate identification of pictures) may be reversed.

V–12a/b

GETTYSBURG: A JOURNEY IN TIME

V–12 a and b Boulders at the eastern face of Devil's Den, Tyson, stereo (a) #585 (b) #540, ca. 1865 (Darrah).

As is evident from both views (here joined, though designed to be viewed separately), the boulders in Devil's Den were enormous and made an ideal bulwark for Confederate sharpshooters. Like many of the terrain features at Gettysburg, the name given this landmark was of local origin and pre-dated the Civil War. Once heavily wooded, Devil's Den was cleared of most of its timber a year or two before the battle, possibly by the same enterprising farmer who cleared the western face of Little Round Top.

The boulders seen here, among the largest in the Den, were quite visible from the Union positions on Little Round Top. Because of their size, it was therefore only natural that Gibson would have selected these very rocks on which to mount his camera to record the distant view of Little Round Top (10). Additionally, one of O'Sullivan's versions of the hill (11) was taken from almost the identical spot on which the Tysons produced these two photographs.

V–12a/b, Modern

V–13

V–14

V–13, Modern   V–14, Modern

V–13 Dead Confederate soldier in the Slaughter Pen, Gibson, stereo #258, July 6, 1863 (LC).

V–14 Confederate dead in the Slaughter Pen, Gardner, stereo #265, July 6, 1863 (LC).

While the fame of Devil's Den has traditionally centered on its Confederate sharpshooters, the struggle preceding the Den's capture by Southern forces—much of it in the area known as the Slaughter Pen, located between Big Round Top and Devil's Den—was nevertheless a fierce one. This area was among the last portions of the entire field to be cleared of its dead, and the photographs taken in this vicinity in turn are among the last Gettysburg views to show fallen soldiers.

The bodies in these two photographs, one of which appears in both Gibson and Gardner versions, were originally identified as "Dead Confederate Soldiers in the Slaughter Pen at the Foot of Round Top." Their exact unit was not specified; conceivably both were members of the 44th Alabama Regiment, killed during the fighting on July 2.

The name "Slaughter Pen" was undoubtedly first heard by Gardner's men or Alfred R. Waud (see 20, 21), a sketch artist for *Harper's Weekly* whom they met in the area, from members of Union burial details. It never caught on, and, for example, will not be heard on the battlefield today. Indeed, its popular use, since 1863, has been limited almost exclusively to the captions for two of the photographs taken by Gardner's men, 15 and 17.

V–15   View in the Slaughter Pen at the foot of Big Round Top, O'Sullivan, plate, July 6, 1863 (NA).

The struggle for Devil's Den began at approximately four-thirty in the afternoon and continued for about an hour and a half. Finally threatened with envelopment, Union forces grudgingly relinquished their position, leaving the entire Den to the Confederates.

Though the Slaughter Pen was occupied by Confederate soldiers for roughly twenty-four hours, the exigencies of battle and the nearby presence of hostile forces did not allow the opportunity to conduct adequate burial operations. Thus when Union burial details first ventured into Devil's Den on July 4, the vast majority of those killed during the second day's fighting, both Union and Confederate, still lay uncovered. Because the initial efforts of the Northern squads were directed toward the interment of their own dead, few Confederate soldiers in this vicinity were buried prior to July 5

V–15

V–15, Modern

V–15, Modern

and July 6.[41] The original caption for O'Sullivan's photograph, taken on the sixth, did not identify the bodies seen strewn amid the rocks. Yet there is little doubt that all are Confederates.

One of the most famous views ever recorded at Gettysburg, O'Sullivan's photograph has, from 1866 until now, been incorrectly identified as a scene at the foot of Little Round Top. Only when field investigation uncovered the split rock appearing at the woodline (left center) was the true whereabouts established.

First misidentified by Gardner himself in the *Sketch Book* (1866), the origin of how Little Round Top came to be associated with this view may actually be traced back to 1863. Gardner, who was naturally unfamiliar with Gettysburg and the surrounding terrain when on the field, did not distinguish between the larger and smaller hills, referring to them both as simply Round Top. The original 1863 title for this scene, "Slaughter Pen, Foot of Round Top" was therefore accurate as far as Gardner knew at the time. Retaining the original title in his *Sketch Book* three years later, Gardner then proceeded to describe the photograph as a scene at the foot of the smaller but more famous of the two hills.

While his error may have been unintentional, there is evidence to suggest that Gardner purposely misinterpreted "Round Top" in order to discuss in his narrative another aspect of the battle more famous than the struggle for Devil's Den. Other discrepancies appear in the *Sketch Book's* Gettysburg captions, some based clearly on fantasy designed to enhance the narrative. In Gardner's defense, we must remember that he was, above all, a photographer and a businessman—not a professional historian.

Why the traditional location for this scene has never before been questioned becomes obvious with a brief glance at the modern version. The woods at the northwestern base of Big Round Top, over the years, have expanded to such an extent that the original scene no longer appears as it did in 1863. Had these woods been limited to their original boundary, the photograph's true location would surely have been detected before now. The two modern versions indicate the problem: the split rock is currently not visible from the original camera position and is only revealed by a close-up view.

V–16   Dead Confederate soldier, Gardner, stereo #229, July 6, 1863 (LC).

Originally entitled "All over now—Confederate sharpshooter at foot of Round Top," the exact position from which this poignant scene was recorded has not been established. Yet based on a familiarity with the locales Gardner is known to have covered, together with a knowledge of the terminology Gardner used to identify these locales, it is reasonably certain that the fallen soldier seen here was photographed somewhere in the Slaughter Pen, along the rock-choked banks of Plum Run.

Bloated, drenched by recent showers, and emitting odors of the most offensive nature, this poor soul had been lying motionless in death for nearly four days when his distorted form attracted the attention of Alexander Gardner. That Gardner was here endeavoring to capture the tragic loneliness of dying on a battlefield far from home is readily apparent. But beyond this, there perhaps is a message of eternal rest and the termination of worldly suffering—a concept expressed in Gardner's original caption, "All over now . . ."

V–17   Scene in the woods at the northwestern base of Big Round Top, Gibson, stereo #252, July 6, 1863 (LC).

V–18   Scene in the woods at the foot of Big Round Top, Gardner, stereo #253, July 6, 1863 (LC).

V–19   Scene in the woods at the foot of Big Round Top, Gibson, stereo #249, July 6, 1863 (LC).

Frequently, when Gardner's crew came upon a body or group of bodies that they considered particularly interesting, several negatives were recorded from different camera positions. This practice added a certain degree of variety to their series, while minimizing the necessity of time-consuming moves from one locale to another.

The three views here constitute one such group of photographs, although they have never before been presented as such. Identified by Gardner as views "in Slaughter Pen, foot of Round Top," all three photographs have

V–17

V–19

V–18

19

18

17

traditionally been placed at the foot of Little Round Top, evidently in accordance with Gardner's use of the name "Slaughter Pen" in his *Sketch Book*. At the time these scenes were recorded, however, "Slaughter Pen, foot of Round Top" meant to Gardner that area bounded by the northwestern foot of Big Round Top and the eastern edge of Devil's Den. Based on the original captions, there is little question that these photographs were taken somewhere inside the woodline seen in view 15, at the foot of Big Round Top—not Little Round Top.

In an effort to locate this point precisely, the photographs have been pieced together by means of the accompanying diagram in the hope that while none of the rocks depicted are outstanding in shape or size, at least the pattern they form may still be discovered. The effort proved futile, for although the lay of the land revealed by the views matches that of Big Round Top's northwestern base, the specific rock pattern could not be found among the numerous formations in the immediate vicinity. A battlefield trolley line was constructed through this very area in the 1890s, and it will never be known exactly how much damage to it was done, nor how many boulders were blasted at that time.

As to the identity of the bodies present in these views, we can only assume, in the absence of caption delineation, that all six are Confederate. As already explained, few if any Northern dead would have been encountered by Gardner's crew on July 6. The fact that at least two of the soldiers are wearing dark uniforms, suggesting Union blue, may be explained by the common practice among Confederate soldiers of wearing clothing in various shades of brown. It is impossible in a black and white photograph to distinguish between dark blue and dark brown, especially when the clothing had been subjected, as this clothing had, to recent rainfall.

V–20

V–21

V–20   Alfred R. Waud, artist for Harper's Weekly, Devil's Den, O'Sullivan, stereo #254, July 6, 1863 (LC).

V–21   The Slaughter Pen as sketched by Alfred Waud, July 6, 1863 (LC).

It is interesting today to contemplate the conversation that must have transpired between Gardner's men and Alfred Waud, sketch artist for *Harper's Weekly*, at the time of their chance meeting in Devil's Den. The fact that O'Sullivan took the trouble to photograph him suggests· that the men knew each other from before, the photograph perhaps a token of their friendship.

Sitting on a boulder situated just several yards from Gardner's camera positions for many of the Slaughter Pen photographs, Waud is here posed gazing northward toward the Valley of Death. The sketch he had been working on when photographed (21) was not produced from this boulder, but rather from another boulder beyond and to the left of the bushes seen in the left background.* That Waud went to great length to portray the Slaughter Pen as accurately as possible is clear from the modern photograph.

Significantly, Waud's handwritten title for the sketch read "Hill where Genl. Weed was killed and ravine from which the rebels were driven by the 3rd Corps, called by the soldiers the Slaughter Pen," indicating the possibility that Waud got the name "Slaughter Pen" from Gardner's crew or vice versa. Several of Waud's Gettysburg sketches were reproduced as woodcuts in *Harper's Weekly* soon after the battle. This particular rendering has remained unpublished until now.

* This conclusion is based on an analysis of Waud's original Gettysburg pencil sketches, which have been preserved by the Library of Congress.

V–22a

V–22b

V–22 a and b   Soldiers posing as bodies in Devil's Den, Weaver, cdv's, o/a November 19, 1863 (NPS, a; LC, b).

Sometime during the late fall of 1863, and most likely on November 19, the day the Soldiers' National Cemetery was formally dedicated (II-16, 17), the Weavers of Hanover, Pennsylvania, recorded a series of no fewer than six *carte de visite* views in Devil's Den, two of which are shown here.

These are posed scenes. Whether the Weavers were deliberately attempting to fool the public into thinking that the soldiers were actually dead is not known. Had this been their purpose, they should have been more discreet about using the identical boulder for two photographs, with the bodies completely rearranged in each. Additionally, the theatrical poses used throughout this series, the healthy appearance of the "corpses," together with the absence of leaves on the trees, all detract considerably from any potential realism the scenes may have offered.

As to where the Weavers encountered the soldiers to pose for them at that time: likely they were participants in the dedication ceremonies, coaxed by fun or profit to accompany the photographers into Devil's Den. (The two men standing amid the "bodies," according to a handwritten notation on one version, are a Dr. Sanford, with the broad-rimmed hat, and a Dr. Leiford, with the cap, both otherwise unidentified.)

V–22a/b. Modern

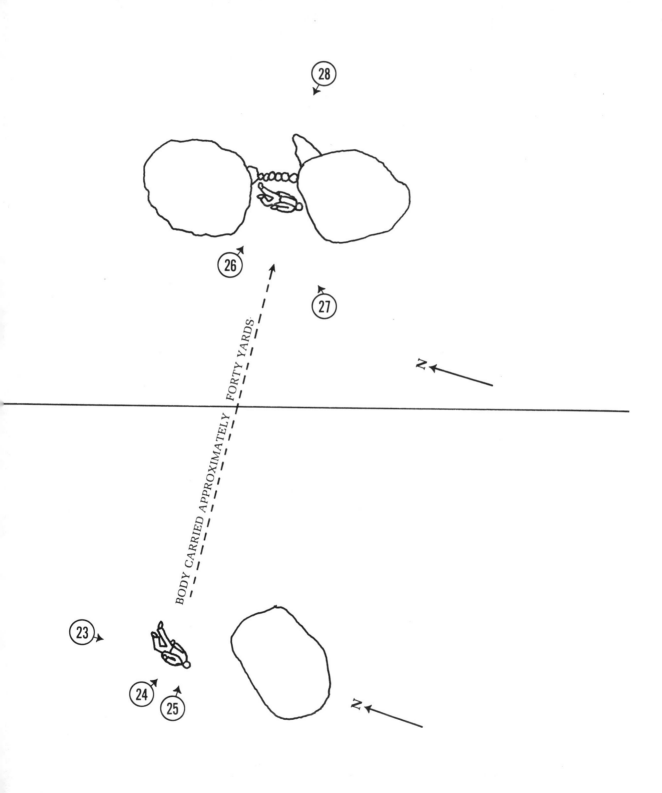

BODY CARRIED APPROXIMATELY FORTY YARDS

V–23 through 26 a and b

The following series of five photographs comprises a record of what is certainly one of the most unusual incidents in the story of photography at Gettysburg: the actual relocation of a dead body some forty yards for the purpose of composing a more effective scene.

V–23   Dead Confederate soldier, Devil's Den, Gardner, stereo #244, July 6, 1863 (LC).

V–24   Dead Confederate soldier, Devil's Den, O'Sullivan, stereo #263, July 6, 1863 (LC).

V–25   Dead Confederate soldier, Devil's Den, Gardner, stereo #277, July 6, 1863 (LC).

Gardner's cameramen first came upon the body of this soldier, probably a member of either the 1st Texas or the 17th Georgia, lying beside a large boulder on the southern slope of Devil's Den. Obviously touched by the age of the youth, Gardner and O'Sullivan proceeded to record four negatives at this location, three of which are reproduced here. That Gardner was attempting, for nearly half an hour, to achieve a sentimental composition from his subject matter is indicated by one of the captions he used to describe the scene: "A sharpshooter's last sleep." (Judging from where the body was found, it is doubtful that the soldier was actually a sharpshooter, but instead an ordinary infantryman, killed while advancing up the slope.)

In the first view (23) the camera is looking southeast. Today the general area where the body was initially photographed is so overgrown that this first view is the only one for which it was possible to secure a modern version—and even this image could not be taken from precisely the same camera position as the original.

In the second photograph (24), looking east, the woods at the Slaughter Pen may be seen in the distant right background. In the third view (25), Gardner turned his camera so as to face in the direction of Little Round Top, hidden by the boulders of Devil's Den. Among the latter rocks is one of particular interest: the rock directly above and to the right of the bush in the center. Adjoining this rock was a stone wall which would serve as the backdrop for the following two views.

V–23

V–24

V–26a

V–26b

V–26 a and b Dead Confederate soldier at sharpshooter's position in Devil's Den, O'Sullivan, (a) plate (b) stereo #251, July 6, 1863 (LC).

After recording the preceding group, Gardner's men moved some forty yards away and were struck by the photographic potential of the scene they found. Here at the stone wall constructed by Southern soldiers sometime on the night of July 2, was the essence of the Den's more famous role in the battle: that of a sharpshooter position for the Confederates. The location itself was ideal, complete with massive boulders, with the wall and even a portion of Little Round Top appearing in the distance. But one vital ingredient necessary for a perfect view was missing. There were no bodies.

In what must have been a flash of creative excitement, the cameramen chose to improvise. Returning to the position they had just photographed, Gardner's men placed the slain youth's body onto a blanket (seen beneath the soldier in O'Sullivan's unsuccessful stereo version, 26b) and in all likelihood carried him themselves some forty yards up the slope.[42] (While it is plausible that they may have solicited aid from members of a nearby

V–26, Modern

burial detail, Gardner generally avoided interfering with the work of weary Union soldiers, who could not have been in the best of spirits at that time, especially for a task such as this.)

To complete their composition, the cameramen propped a rifle (definitely not the type used by sharpshooters) against the wall and placed a knapsack under the soldier's head. The purpose of the knapsack was to support a story apparently formulated as Gardner pondered the scene's potential. According to his *Sketch Book*, this soldier, described as a sharpshooter, was wounded at the stone wall by a shell fragment, whereupon the dying boy evidently laid himself down to stoically await his end. The lengthy caption continues by telling how Gardner returned to the spot four months later to find the body, then a skeleton, and the rusted rifle, both undisturbed— an obvious case of fiction. (The body would have been long since buried, and the rifle would have been picked up either by Union forces or relic hunters. Significantly, only one such weapon appears in any single Gardner view, suggesting that the identical rifle may have been used as a prop throughout Gardner's Gettysburg series.)

When one considers that Gardner's crew must have expended approximately a full hour on this one body—they photographed it a total of six times and at two different locations—the possibility clearly arises that this may have been one of the last bodies photographed at Gettysburg. Perhaps new subject matter was getting exceedingly scarce as burial operations drew to a close.

The photographer's efforts were nevertheless well spent, for out of these six views emerged one of the most memorable of all Gettysburg photographs—the fallen "sharpshooter" by the wall (26a). Although Gardner claimed credit for this view in his *Sketch Book*, the original catalogue issued only two months following the battle identified the cameraman as O'Sullivan.

V–27 Confederate sharpshooter position in Devil's Den, view looking east, Tyson, stereo #546, ca. 1865 (Darrah).

V–28 Sharpshooter position, Devil's Den, view looking west, Tyson, stereo #541, ca. 1865 (Darrah).

Whether or not the Tyson decision to take these two views was stimulated by O'Sullivan's dramatic photograph is of course unknown. But because this sharpshooter position was the most distinctive in Devil's Den, the chances are great that the Tysons made their selection independently.

The condition of the wall and the growth of weeds show that a year or two had elapsed before the Tyson scenes were recorded. (The young pine tree seen to the left in the first view (27) does not appear in O'Sullivan's photographs because of O'Sullivan's camera position.) The second Tyson view (28) was taken looking west from the opposite side of the wall and in the direction from which Confederate forces advanced. Northern infantrymen, well-positioned behind boulders such as those seen here, were able to offer a stiff resistance during the early stages of the struggle for the

V–27

V–28

V–27, Modern

V–28, Modern

GETTYSBURG: A JOURNEY IN TIME

Den, but eventually succumbed to overwhelming numbers and pressure on their left flank from the 44th Alabama Regiment.

Barely visible just above the stone wall in view 28 is the distant barn of the Timbers farm. The Timbers, like the Bryans (IV-3), were free blacks who fled their home prior to the battle. Though the Timbers house and barn are no longer standing, the foundations remain and may be inspected after a short excursion into the woods that currently cover much of the ground seen in the distant background of the Tyson view of the Confederate sharpshooter position.

Eventually reconstructed, the stone wall situated on the southern summit of Devil's Den is today preserved by the National Park Service as a silent reminder of the Den's tragic role during the battle.

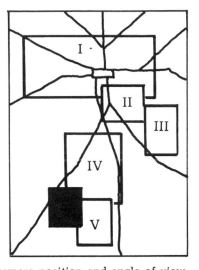

Original camera position and angle of view.

Approximate vicinity in which view was recorded; precise location not determined.

Union infantry regiment.

Confederate infantry regiment.

I

II

III

IV

V

N

0

SCALE

MILES

1/8

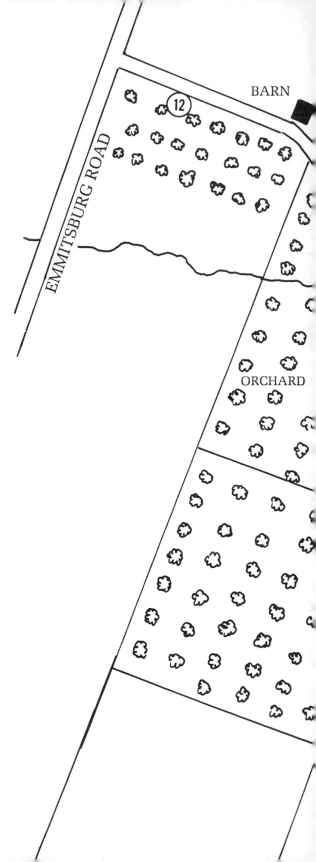

EMMITSBURG ROAD

BARN

12

ORCHARD

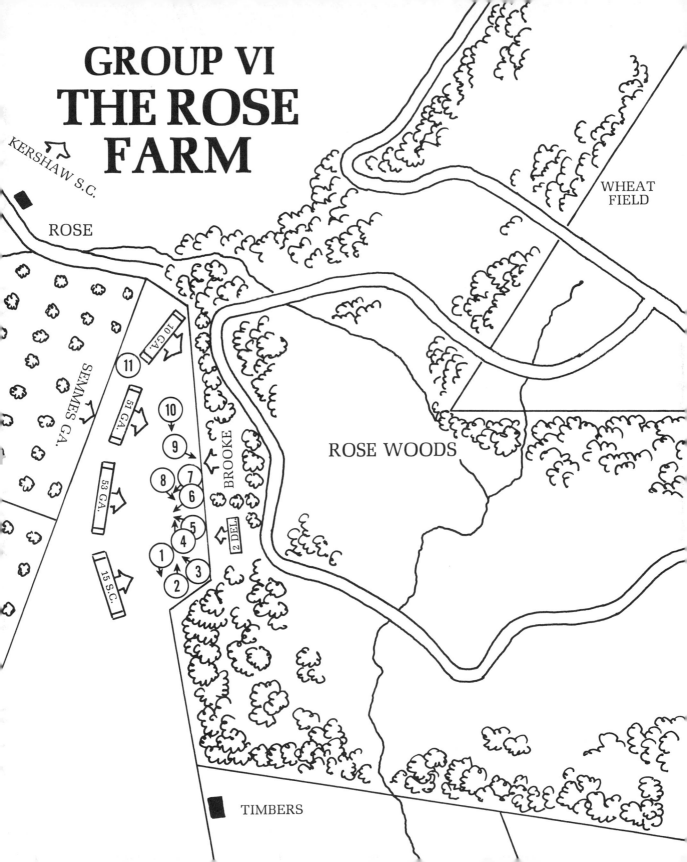

GROUP VI
THE ROSE FARM

KERSHAW S.C.

ROSE

WHEAT FIELD

SEMMES GA.

10 GA.

⑪

51 GA.

⑩

⑨

53 GA.

⑧ ⑦

BROOKE

⑥

ROSE WOODS

⑤

④

2 DEL.

① ③

②

15 S.C.

TIMBERS

14

GROUP VI: THE ROSE FARM

The following series of photographs—1 through 10—contains some of the most dramatic and best-known battlefield scenes ever recorded. They are accurately identified here for the first time.

While several views in this group are today quite rare, the more famous have been individually labeled over the past century as showing Union dead at McPherson's Woods (near Lee's headquarters, to the west of town), Confederate dead on the first day's field, Union dead near the scene of Pickett's charge, and dead soldiers gathered for burial in the area known as the Wheatfield (to the far south of town). Yet a close study of the photographs shows, in fact, that they are views of the same bodies.

In all, ten different Gardner scenes (one photographed twice, both in plate form and as a stereo, thus making eleven negatives) were eventually linked to this one location, their interrelationship portrayed in the accompanying diagram.

It was Gardner's intention to give each of the views a distinctive quality by alternating backgrounds. Utilizing the woods and adjoining open fields to maximum advantage, his cameramen were able to achieve variety in composition without relocating their darkroom equipment. As a result of these efforts, the photographs have long been viewed as if each was entirely separate from the others, a practice which in effect has eliminated the possibility of determining the scene's location.

In 1962, guided by traditional captions, the pattern of rocks, and the outstanding panorama created when the backgrounds are joined, I began a search to discover this location. Initially, I considered McPherson's Woods the most likely site, for not only had a number of the views been traditionally placed on the first day's field, but the northern edge of those woods matched the total background pattern quite well.

But what could not be explained was the presence of numerous rocks in the photographs—none was to be found at the edge of McPherson's Woods, either in 1863 or today. One rock in particular (see 8) was vitally important in establishing beyond a doubt the scene's location.

Disregarding tradition, I began a systematic search of the entire twenty-five square mile battlefield. The search took five long years, and ended successfully only in March of 1967, after what seemed like endless frustration. But once the precise location was discovered, there could be no question. Using the previously mentioned rock as a reference point, everything instantly fell into place—the other less distinctive rocks, the background pattern, even Gardner's original captions, which until then had been too vague to be of any use.

What is here depicted is not McPherson's Woods, nor the famous Wheatfield, nor any of the traditional locations, but instead an out-of-the-way field adjoining the southwestern edge of the Rose Woods, in the general area of Devil's Den, nearly three miles south of the McPherson farm.

Once the location became clear, it then followed that far from showing the first day's field, all ten photographs actually showed thirty-four Confederate soldiers killed during the second day's battle. The specific action began slightly after six o'clock on the evening of July 2, when Brigadier General Paul J. Semmes's Georgia brigade, moving in support of a South Carolina brigade already engaged (led by Brigadier General Joseph B. Kershaw), advanced eastward through the Rose Woods and into the famous Wheatfield beyond. Just as these fresh Confederate reinforcements entered the southern portion of the Wheatfield, they were confronted with a stiff Union counterattack, spearheaded by the brigade of Colonel John R. Brooke (whose five regiments were understrength because of losses incurred at the battle of Chancellorsville). Pushing the Southerners back before them, Brooke's men, their bayonets fixed, stormed into the Rose Woods and seized the rocky ledge situated within the southwestern woodline. At this point, the Northerners halted to re-form their ranks and prepare for the enemy counterattack.

Driven back across the field depicted in the photographs to follow, Semmes's center and right flank units, the 10th, 51st, and 53rd Georgia, together with the 15th South Carolina, which in the confusion of battle had become separated from the remainder of Kershaw's brigade, positioned themselves behind a stone wall some two hundred yards west of the woods.

Within moments, the Confederate battle line, its flags waving and its soldiers shrieking the rebel yell, scrambled over the wall and swept across the open ground to their front, to be met by a murderous volley of enemy fire from the Rose Woods. It was during this encounter that the Confederate soldiers seen in these photographs were killed.

For nearly fifteen minutes the bloody struggle continued as Colonel Brooke, his depleted brigade now isolated from all other Union forces, desperately awaited support.

Realizing the precarious nature of their foe's position, the Southerners advanced one last time in an effort to envelop Brooke's line. The pressure was too great to bear, and reluctantly the five Union regiments relinquished their hold on the woodline and fell back into the confusion of the Wheatfield.

By this time, the Northern positions originally established by General Sickles were rapidly disintegrating at all points, Little Round Top alone ultimately staving off Union disaster on the southern extreme of the field.

That the bodies appearing in the ten photographs are all Confederate is supported by several factors. Without exception, Gardner's original captions identify them as Confederates; distinctive Southern uniforms appear throughout the various clusters of dead; Brooke's line did not fight beyond the woodline—thus none of the Union soldiers actually fell in the open field to the southwest;[43] and finally, these same bodies are mentioned, and described as being Confederate, in accounts written by members of the Pennsylvania Reserve brigade, which, with little opposition, recaptured the southwestern edge of the Rose Woods late on the evening of July 3. According to these accounts, the bodies found in this open field had been laid out for burial by Southern comrades who, with the arrival of the Pennsylvanians, were forced to abandon their work prior to completion.[44]

Because subsequent Union burial details concerned themselves mainly with the interment of Union dead on July 4 and July 5, these fallen soldiers were consequently left untouched from July 3 until July 5, the date on which their bloated forms were captured forever through the medium of photography.

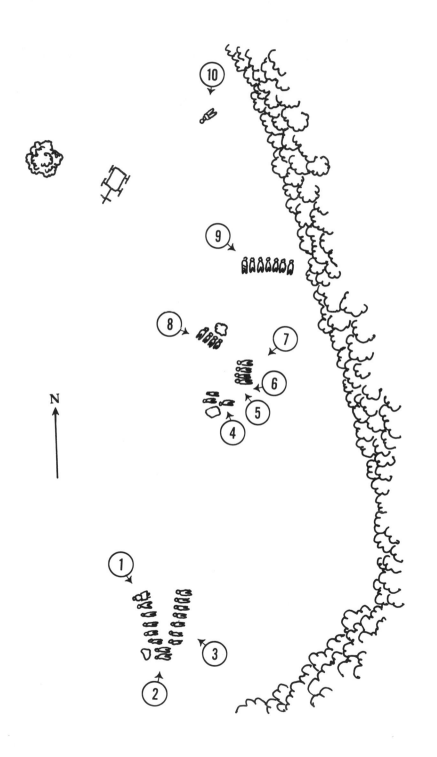

VI–1 Confederate dead gathered for burial at the southwestern edge of the Rose Woods, O'Sullivan, stereo #245, July 5, 1863 (LC).

VI–2 Confederate dead at the edge of the Rose Woods, O'Sullivan, stereo #227, July 5, 1863 (LC).

VI–3 Confederate dead, view looking toward the orchard on the Rose farm, O'Sullivan, stereo #260, July 5, 1863 (LC).

The bodies seen gathered into a "V" formation in each of these photographs are identical.

Few, if any, of the early Gettysburg views have ever received greater fame than the first of this group (1). Traditionally identified as being dead of the Union Iron Brigade (more specifically, of the 24th Michigan) killed during the first day's battle at McPherson's Woods, the bodies here depicted are in reality Confederate soldiers, probably members of either the 15th South Carolina or 53rd Georgia regiments, killed on July 2, at the Rose Woods, almost three miles south of the McPherson farm. The camera was pointing southeast, away from the town.

Originally, Gardner entitled the view simply "A Harvest of Death." This caption was retained for several years after the battle. But when the Civil War views were reissued during the 1880s, someone evidently felt the need for a more precise historical identification, perhaps to meet the demands of an audience by then sufficiently familiar with the various landmarks on the Gettysburg battlefield. In any case, the photograph was quite arbitrarily identified as "Bodies of the dead collected for burial in the field near McPherson's Woods, south of Chambersburg Pike, on battlefield of first day." It was a safe caption, for although neither this scene, nor any of the nine taken nearby, appears in Gardner's *Sketch Book*, the book clearly established Gardner's presence on the first day's field. Furthermore, when one compares the background of this view to Brady's documented panorama of McPherson's Woods (I-2), the fence visible in both seems to be identical.

Immediately accepted as a view at McPherson's Woods, it was then not long before some observant editor noticed the dark broad-rimmed hat seen covering the face of one of the bodies to the right. As chance would have it, hats such as this, common in the Confederate army, were also worn by members of the Union Iron Brigade. Obviously, because the scene was supposed to have been taken at or near McPherson's Woods, and since the Iron Brigade wore hats of the type depicted here, it appeared only logical

VI–1

to conclude that these soldiers must have been members of the Iron Brigade. From that conclusion it was deduced that the specific regiment must have been the Iron Brigade's renowned 24th Michigan, possibly because this regiment suffered 80 percent casualties during the first day's fighting. Thus by 1911, when Miller's mammoth ten-volume *Photographic History of the Civil War* was first published, the compounded error had already been established as fact, not to be refuted until now.

Today, the southwestern edge of the Rose Woods, a rarely visited but nonetheless memorable portion of the battlefield, bears little resemblance to its 1863 appearance. The woods themselves, as is revealed by the modern version for the first view, have expanded beyond their original boundary. Additionally, a considerable portion of the foreground has been gouged out by erosion. Erosion has also eaten away the ground at the base of one of the two rocks visible in the background of the original, making that rock (center of view) look larger today than it did at the time of the battle.

The second photograph (2), traditionally misidentified as a scene at McPherson's Woods, was recorded with the camera facing northward, the Rose Woods dominating the right background.

VI–2

VI–3

In the third scene (3), traditionally miscaptioned as a view in the famous Wheatfield, the camera was facing toward the northwest with the Rose Woods to the photographer's back. The angle is the line of vision of Brooke's left flank unit, the 2nd Delaware Infantry, looking out on the open field over which the 15th South Carolina and 53rd Georgia regiments advanced during their counterattack against Brooke's line. Visible in the distant background are some of the trees of John Rose's peach orchard. The Rose house itself is hidden by the large tree on the right horizon; a portion of Rose's barn roof may be detected to the immediate left of that same tree.

Because bodies were usually buried within several yards of where they fell, large groups of dead gathered for interment, such as the group depicted in this "V" formation, indicate specific areas in which unusually heavy casualties were sustained. It should be mentioned that for every man killed in action during Civil War battles, roughly four were wounded.

Understandably wary about touching the corpses, the Confederate sol-

206

diers who gathered them for burial on July 3 tied ropes or belts around the limbs of several before dragging or carrying them to this formation. These appendages are clearly visible on the legs, and in some cases on the wrists of a few of the bodies.

Due to the subsequent erosion of the ground at this locale, the modern versions for the second two views were taken from a slightly lower elevation. The camera angles and backgrounds, however, are identical to those present in each of O'Sullivan's two originals.

Left, VI–1, Modern
Below left, VI–2, Modern
Below right, VI–3, Modern

VI–4

VI–5

VI–4 **Confederate dead gathered for burial at the edge of the Rose Woods, Gardner, stereo #256, July 5, 1863 (LC).**

VI–5 **Confederate dead gathered for burial, Gardner, stereo #268, July 5, 1863 (LC).**

Of particular interest in the two scenes reproduced here is the presence of Gardner's darkroom wagon on the horizon. (It may also be seen in 2, taken from a slightly different perspective.)

Upon close inspection, an extension is visible protruding from the back step of the wagon. It was here, inside a light-proof well, that the negatives for these scenes were processed.

The darkroom wagon is without its horses. No doubt the photographers realized they were going to spend a good portion of the afternoon at this one locale, and unhitched the team to graze somewhere nearby.

In both photographs, the camera was pointed facing northward in the direction of the famous Sherfy Peach Orchard. (The Sherfy orchard, never specifically photographed by any of the early cameramen, was the scene of considerable action on July 2. It has generally come to be known simply as the "Peach Orchard.") It was in support of Kershaw's South Carolinians, then engaged with Union forces positioned in the orchard, that Semmes's brigade initially advanced on the evening of July 2.

Despite traditional captions, which for some reason have long identified both these scenes as dead of the 1st Minnesota (a famous Union regiment that fought on a portion of the battlefield one mile to the northeast), the fallen soldiers seen here were probably members of Semmes's 51st and 53rd Georgia regiments, or Kershaw's 15th South Carolina Regiment, the only outfits to suffer significant casualties at this specific point.

VI–4, Modern

VI–5, Modern

VI–6

VI–7

VI–6 Dead Confederate soldiers, view looking toward Seminary Ridge, O'Sullivan, stereo #257, July 5, 1863 (LC).

VI–7 Confederate dead gathered for burial, view looking toward Seminary Ridge, O'Sullivan, stereo #239, July 5, 1863 (LC).

Taken just several feet apart, but looking in the same southwestern direction, these two photographs provide a unique visual record of the ground over which Lee's right flank units advanced during the second day's battle. Clearly visible traversing the far background is the southern extension of Seminary Ridge (also known in this area as Warfield Ridge), the position from which the Confederate brigades of Law, Robertson, Kershaw, and Semmes (among others) commenced their assaults.

The backgrounds of the views here complement each other ideally and may be joined at the pair of large trees appearing in the middle distance. These same trees are situated at the stone wall where Semmes's brigade re-formed its line and began the final advance toward the camera position.

Of interest is the presence in the first version (6) of the soldier lying against the rock, and his absence from the second (7). The fact that he was moved probably indicates that a Union burial detail had reached the scene before Gardner's crew finished taking their last negatives. In all likelihood the body was placed inside the grave beside the soldier with the raised knee moments after O'Sullivan's first version was recorded. (The grave is also visible in views 4 and 5, as is the soldier with the raised knee. It is doubtful, in this instance, that the cameramen relocated the body, for it would have served little or no purpose and would not have been worth the effort.) One method of burial employed on Civil War battlefields was to dig a grave, place a body in the open hole, dig an adjoining grave, cover the first with the dirt from the second, and so forth until an entire row or cluster of bodies was interred. This method may have been the one being used here.

Left, VI–6, Modern
Right, VI–7, Modern

VI-8

VI–8 Confederate dead at the edge of the Rose Woods, view looking south-east, Gardner, stereo #235, July 5, 1863 (LC).

One of the lesser known of the ten different scenes recorded along the edge of the Rose Woods, this view is by far the most significant, for without the presence of the distinctive split rock visible in the right background, none of the ten photographs would ever have been located.

As was typical of Gardner's vague 1863 captions, this scene was originally entitled simply "Confederate soldiers as they fell near the centre of the battlefield." Because the nine companion captions were equally vague, in some cases contradicting each other by describing the identical ground as being both on the "Confederate right wing" (4) and at the "Confederate centre" (9), the precise meaning of Gardner's terminology was elusive to say the least. What did "centre" mean in this case? What part of the battlefield? On what day? Most important, did Gardner actually know what he was talking about?

The rock held the answer—though the difficulty and frustration of finding it may be gleaned when one considers that there are literally tens of thousands of rocks scattered about the twenty-five square miles of battlefield, not to mention the changes in terrain due to erosion and foliage growth. As is readily apparent from the modern photograph, the location of this scene was by no means obvious. Since the split rock is today partially hidden from the original camera position by latter-day trees, a close-up view is included.

VI–8, Modern

VI−9

VI−9, Modern

VI–9 Confederate dead, view at the edge of the Rose Woods, Gibson, stereo #246, July 5, 1863 (LC).

This view is the only Rose Woods photograph definitely known to have been taken by James Gibson, suggesting that most of Gibson's time in that area was probably spent processing plates at the nearby darkroom wagon.

Traditionally misidentified as bodies gathered for burial near McPherson's Woods on the first day's field, the soldiers seen here are identical to those in the right background of Gardner view 4. At first glance, these seven bodies seem quite typical of the bodies in the other photographs. Yet an unusual fact appears when one studies the body closest to the camera in 9. As is confirmed by the Gardner scene, his trousers have been pulled below the hips, revealing his buttocks. An odd topic for discussion, admittedly, but the fact deserves explanation.

It will have been noted that most of the fallen soldiers photographed at Gettysburg were severely bloated. This bloating was the result of gas generated by decomposition, a process that took place rapidly during the warm summer days of early July. At times the internal pressures created were great enough to force open the buttons on the trouser fronts (see for example 3, 4). Thus the trousers on the soldier seen here were most likely open before his body was dragged to this position, the dragging action forcing them down below his hips.

Here then was a young man who, only three days prior, advanced into battle, full of life, and presumably fighting for ideals he considered worthy of noble sacrifice. But by July 5, on the field at Gettysburg, he was just another nameless corpse, his face pressed against the earth, his exposed buttocks, once carefully hidden in accordance with the vanities of civilization, a sign of war's ultimate glory.

Today the ground on which these seven bodies were first buried appears much as it did in 1863. Even the oval rock at the far end of the line of bodies (not visible in the modern photograph) may still be seen by the modern visitor. That rock, heavier than it looks, is currently imbedded upside down in the earth, its distinctive markings unchanged by time.

VI–10 Dead Confederate soldier, view in field adjoining the Rose Woods, Gardner, stereo #274, July 5, 1863 (LC).

While an eight-by-ten-inch version of this scene, the only large plate recorded at the Rose Woods, has been reproduced in a number of past works, the more spatially revealing stereo view is presented here for the first time. Due to the slightly telescopic nature of the lens used on the eight-by-ten-inch camera, the larger version, though taken from the identical position, does not in fact show the entire background, focusing instead all attention on the dead soldier; and without this background, the connection of this scene with the other nine views could never have been established. The two rocks in the left distance both appear in several of the preceding photographs, and the rail fence (to the immediate right of the two rocks) is the same one seen in O'Sullivan's famous view of the "V" formation (1). (Additionally, the body itself may be detected as an indistinct white form beyond and to the left of the rock in the center of view 4.)

Originally identified as "War, effect of a shell on a Confederate soldier," Gardner obviously tried to increase the impact of his composition by placing an artillery shell on the ground above the soldier's right knee, and by laying a rifle across both legs. Note also the soldier's dismembered hand to the front of the rifle.

Like most of the other bodies photographed at the southwestern edge of the Rose Woods, the man seen here was probably a member of Semmes's brigade. He lies on the ground over which the 51st and 53rd Georgia regiments advanced during their July 2 assault against the woodline. Although his name was recorded somewhere on his unit's casualty report, he eventually was buried by enemy soldiers in an unmarked grave, and his identity as an individual will forever remain unknown.

The loss is one we share. There is nothing quite like a name to impart the personalized horror of war. Without a name it is all too easy to view this mutilated corpse as an object; as merely one of the countless reminders that war is, in the final analysis, the most disgusting of obscenities.

And yet this object was a human being. As a typical member of Semmes's brigade he was probably born in Georgia during the early 1840s. Growing to adolescence during the 1850s, he must have viewed the gathering political storm with the detachment of youth, concerning himself more with the chores and pleasures of his own personal world.

Then came the war, the great adventure. In life, this soldier probably

VI–10, Modern

posed before the camera wearing a new uniform, his face flushed with determined pride, a hand grasping the barrel of a rifle, ready to defend the honor of his homeland against the Yankee horde.

Perhaps he was Private Gideon B. Thomas of Early County's Company A, 51st Georgia Regiment; or Private Wiley J. Moss of Newton County's Company B, 53rd Georgia Regiment, both members of Semmes's brigade killed at Gettysburg, both buried in unmarked graves.

The young man seen here has undoubtedly been perceived countless times over the past century as a vague nonentity, a corpse more awesome and revolting than real. We may look upon this photograph with disgust and say to ourselves, "War is horrible." But we quickly forget.

Somewhere down in Georgia, at the very moment Gardner's negative was being exposed, a family anxiously awaited news of this soldier's fate, hoping he had survived yet another battle unscathed. For that family, the true horror of war would never be forgotten.

VI–11   Confederate dead, probably on or near the Rose farm, O'Sullivan, stereo #236, July 5, 1863 (LC).

In the absence of any distinctive topographical feature, and because none of these bodies appears in other Gardner photographs, the precise location of this view has not been established. On the other hand, Gardner's original caption, "Confederate soldiers who had evidently been shelled by our batteries on Round Top," provides description enough to indicate a general locale. The reference to Round Top indicates that one of the two hills, probably the larger, was likely visible from the camera position. Also, Gardner would not have relocated his entire darkroom set-up just to record one negative, so it is only reasonable to conclude that this scene must have been produced close to an area in which Gardner's crew is known to have worked.

Judging from the general terrain, one may surmise that the photograph was taken somewhere in the fields southwest of the Rose Woods, far enough from that woodline for at least one of the Round Tops to be observed.

The idea that these men were killed by artillery fire was undoubtedly suggested by the body nearest the tree, which bears a gaping wound similar to the one suffered by the soldier in the preceding photograph.

VI–12

GETTYSBURG: A JOURNEY IN TIME

VI–12 Unfinished Confederate grave, probably on the Rose farm, O'Sullivan, stereo #233, July 5, 1863 (LC).

As with the preceding photograph, the scene reproduced here has not been precisely located. But once again a general locale may be approximated.

This scene was originally entitled "Unfinished Confederate grave near the centre of the battlefield." Reference to the "centre" was made in only four other Gardner captions: the view at Trostle's house (IV-4) and three of the Rose Woods photographs (3, 8, 9). Because Gardner's scenes of fallen soldiers had terminated before reaching the Trostle farm, the reference to "centre" here is likely in accord with Gardner's use of the word with regard to the Rose Wood photographs, so it seems that the view was taken somewhere on or close to the Rose farm.

Additional evidence is found in the manuscript records of Confederate burial sites compiled by a local Gettysburg physician during the early days following the battle.[45] These records reveal that on the southern portion of the battlefield, near areas where Gardner worked, most of the Confederate graves marked by individual headboards—as are the graves here—were located in the orchard, yard, and fields surrounding the Rose house and barn. The headboards mean that graves were dug by fellow Confederates.

Indeed, the concentration of Confederate headboards in this photograph, the presence of the peach tree, possibly part of Rose's orchard, and even the whitewashed board fence, typical of those found near buildings rather than in open fields, all suggest that the view was probably recorded in close proximity to either Rose's house or the barn. Both buildings served as Southern hospitals from late on July 2 until evacuated the next evening. If the dead soldiers seen here were photographed in that vicinity, the chances are that they died of wounds shortly after being brought to the hospital and then were buried by their comrades.

The army wagons in the background of this view are being used in conjunction with general cleanup operations, such as the gathering of arms and equipment left on the field by the wounded and the dead.

VI—13 a and b, 14 To repeat, Gardner's prime interest at Gettysburg was in photographing the dead. Because his approach to Gettysburg via the Emmitsburg Road immediately placed him on one of the last portions of the field to be cleared of its dead, Gardner was understandably content to spend most of his time in that vicinity. From a documentary standpoint, he did not cover the field well. And yet, since Gardner obviously knew what he was after, we can only conclude that he was at least initially satisfied with the results; although he had visited relatively few different areas, he had produced a large number of dramatic death studies.

Traditionally, it has been believed that some of these studies were taken at McPherson's Woods on the first day's field. It is my belief that all his photographs showing human dead were recorded in two areas only: on or near the Rose farm, and at Devil's Den. The confusion stems from Gardner's 1863 catalogue.

For the majority of the almost sixty Gettysburg titles listed in that publication, Gardner did make an honest effort to describe the views' locations to the best of his knowledge (understandably limited). Typical of his identifications were "View in Slaughter Pen, foot of Round Top" (V–17), "Scene in a wheatfield on the Confederate right" (2), "View in wheatfield opposite our extreme left" (7), and "View on left" (6). At least in 1863, Gardner, for the most part, was not attempting to fool anyone.

But of all the titles listed in the 1863 catalogue, one—and only one—stands out as odd. Identified as a "View in the field on the right wing where General Reynolds fell," this photograph (13b), an eight-by-ten-inch plate showing several dead soldiers, was the only view in Gardner's entire Gettysburg series to be captioned in the 1863 catalogue as a scene taken on the first day's field.

Two stereo versions of the identical view also appear in the catalogue. But significantly enough, their identifications made no mention of General Reynolds. The stereo captions read simply "View in field on right wing" (13a) and "Federal soldiers as they fell."

Additionally, a pair of companion photographs, though not identified as such, were recorded of these same bodies from a completely different camera position and at an angle of roughly 135° clockwise from the other three views. (That the bodies were identical is demonstrated—for the first time—by the diagram on page 223.) The first of the two companion scenes was an eight-by-ten-inch plate entitled "A Harvest of Death" (14). The

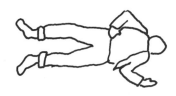

second, identical to the first except in stereo form, was listed as "Evidence of how severe the contest had been on the right." Again, no mention was made of General Reynolds.

Yet, considered together, the two groups of photographs afforded a good basis for determining where the scene was located. But at no point on the entire first day's field, either west or north of town, could the two groups be convincingly matched to the terrain, even with possible contour changes and foliage growth taken into account. Then, with the eventual discovery of the true location for the series recorded at the Rose Woods (1 through 10), it became increasingly clear that, in fact, Gardner's men had never set foot on the first day's field.

Assuming for the moment that they had: if one considers the date of their arrival in the Gettysburg area, and the time they necessarily had to spend in taking the views they did, then the afternoon of July 7 is the earliest Gardner would have reached the area north or west of town. And by that time the last of the dead in those areas had already been buried. Furthermore, in order to reach the first day's field, Gardner could not have avoided passing either the Lutheran Theological Seminary or Pennsylvania College, the two most imposing architectural features at Gettysburg, but neither of which he photographed. It might be argued that Gardner did not photograph either building because he took little interest in such subjects, but why then did he expend two negatives on the comparatively dull Fahnestock building (I–15)? The only persuasive conclusion is that Gardner's crew did not venture beyond the town of Gettysburg.

Indeed, of all the photographs recorded by Gardner's men at Gettysburg, not one depicts a single feature which can definitely be connected with the first day's field (except of course for the Fahnestock building, located in the town itself). Conversely, every view that has been located precisely was taken in an area other than the actual scene of the first day's battle. And every identifiable photograph of fallen soldiers was taken either in the Rose farm area or at Devil's Den.

Why then was one of Gardner's photographs described as a "View in the field on the right wing where General Reynolds fell" in the original 1863 catalogue? I suggest the following explanation.

Because Gardner's men were the only photographers to reach the battlefield before the dead had been buried (and because photographs showing death and destruction were Gardner's prime concern), the cameramen did not linger long after taking their fill of such views. By July 7, the day they began their return trip to Washington, Gardner's crew had succeeded in scooping all the other photographers, specifically Mathew Brady.

But then, as the story of the battle unfolded in the press during the following month, the public quickly learned of the battle's highlights. Two participants in particular arose as national heroes almost overnight: the aged John Burns and the gallant General Reynolds. One can only imagine Gardner's reaction to the August 22, 1863, issue of *Harper's Weekly* which featured eleven Brady photographs reproduced as woodcuts, including views of Pennsylvania College (I–12), General Lee's headquarters (I–6), John Burns (I–13), and the "Wheatfield in which General Reynolds was shot" (I–2)!

Gardner and his crew had photographed none of these famous scenes. In fact, Gardner was probably not even aware of their existence, or at least their significance while at Gettysburg. Unlike Brady, he arrived on the field too soon after the fighting to have had a competent guide. So ironically, although Brady's series was recorded a week or so after Gardner's, it was Brady who finally scooped Gardner by presenting to the public, through the medium of the widely circulated *Harper's Weekly*, some of the first views of famous features on the Gettysburg battlefield. Not until 1865 would any of Gardner's Gettysburg photographs be reproduced as woodcuts in any of the illustrated weeklies.

In September 1863, Gardner's *Catalogue of Photographic Incidents of the War* was first published; and it is my suggestion that for the sake of competition, Gardner hastily selected one of his views which looked as if it might have been taken near Brady's "Wheatfield," and changed the original caption "View in field on right wing" by adding to it—"where General Reynolds fell." Since there was no way Gardner could have changed any of his other titles to come up with a Pennsylvania College, a John Burns, or a Lee's headquarters, he confined his title alterations to the one view, and selected only the eight-by-ten-inch version because the larger lens had conveniently cut out most of the potentially incriminatory background present in the stereo versions.

By the time Gardner's *Sketch Book* was published (1866), the title read simply "Field where General Reynolds Fell," in imitation of Brady's original "Wheatfield" caption. By so doing, Gardner unwittingly copied a minor error. Reynolds did not fall in the field photographed by Brady. Reynolds did not fall in a field at all, but rather inside the eastern edge of McPherson's

Woods (I–4). Whatever, Gardner's photograph portrays an area nowhere near the scene.

Unfortunately, this particular story does not have a completely satisfying conclusion. I have never been able to establish beyond a doubt even an approximate location of these two groups of Gardner photographs (therefore they will not be found on the map for group VI). But I have, I may say, searched every conceivable portion of the battlefield several times (including the scene of the cavalry fight three miles east of town), and my considered guess is that this specific point was situated somewhere in the open fields on the southern extreme of the field, near the Rose farm and close to the Emmitsburg Road. Regretfully, much of this area is today wooded.

VI–13 a and b Union dead at Gettysburg (a) Gibson, stereo #243 (b) O'Sullivan, plate, July 5, 1863 (LC).

Photographs 13a and b are two of the three views Gardner's team took from the same camera position. The most revealing of the three, 13a, is the stereo version originally entitled "View in field on right wing." Considering Gardner's use of the term "right" in all his localizable identifications, it seems probable to suppose that he was referring here to the Confederate right flank of July 2 and 3.

The companion stereo version entitled "Federal soldiers as they fell," not included here, was identical to the first except for the absence of the burial detail members in the middle distance. The arrival of this burial squad probably forced Gardner to seek other subjects, for it is unlikely that the soldiers would have agreed to stop their work and pose more than once.

Of the three versions recorded from this position, O'Sullivan's eight-by-ten-inch plate, 13b, eventually became the most famous. Due to the nature of the lens used with the larger plate-holding camera, little of the background was included, all attention instead being focused on the bodies themselves. Had Gardner not added General Reynolds's name to this one caption, it is doubtful that McPherson's Woods would ever have been associated with any of Gardner's Gettysburg views.

That all the bodies in this group are nevertheless Union soldiers is fairly certain. Not only are they described as such by one of the captions but their uniforms are distinctly Northern as well.

Note also that the shoes on these dead have in each case been removed,

VI–13b

VI–13a

which indicates that wherever this site was, it was at one time situated behind Confederate lines. To compensate for supply shortages, Southern soldiers made a common practice of relieving enemy dead of sorely needed items such as shoes.

Of further interest in this scene is the article of clothing rumpled on the ground to the far right (next to the dead soldier with his arm over his head in 13a). Clearly visible against the dark coloring is what appears to be the diamond-shaped badge worn exclusively by soldiers of the Union Third Corps. Under the command of General Sickles, the Third Corps was engaged on the Union left flank (Confederate right) and suffered heavy casualties at Devil's Den, the Rose farm, and along the Emmitsburg Road.

VI–14   Union dead at Gettysburg, O'Sullivan, plate, July 5, 1863 (NA).

The bodies seen here are identical to those that appear in the preceding two photographs, 13a and b. The camera has been relocated, and we are now looking in a direction roughly 135° clockwise from the first group of views.

Like most of Gardner's scenes showing a cluster of bodies, the individual views, taken looking in various directions, were not intended to be linked together. Thus when both this view, originally entitled "A Harvest of Death," and the plate version of the preceding scene were reproduced in the *Sketch Book*, they were described as two completely different subjects. In one instance (14) the bodies were identified as Confederates, no mention being made of where the view was taken; and in the other (13b), they were identified as Union dead on the first day's field. This contradiction may have been a lapse of memory on Gardner's part. More likely it was deliberate. And the misidentification has remained until the present day.

VI–14

PART FOUR
CONCLUSION

15

THE EARLY PHOTOGRAPHS: A PLEA FOR REAPPRAISAL

No other war prior to the twentieth century was as well documented photographically as was the American Civil War; and of all the battlefields of that war, none was as well documented as Gettysburg.

The credit for this achievement, as should now be clear, belongs not to one man but to many. Gardner, O'Sullivan, Gibson, Brady, the Tysons, the Weavers, Gutekunst, and all their assistants, came to Gettysburg from far and near, and at different times. Some took many views, others took few; some traversed the entire field, others chose to work within limited areas. Alexander Gardner, and his team, the only photographers to reach the field before the dead had been buried, interpreted Gettysburg as they saw it in early July, in a manner quite different from the later interpretations of Mathew Brady and Charles and Isaac Tyson. And yet despite all the many differences between one artist and the other, there had emerged, by 1866, an amazingly well-balanced photographic record of great historic interest.

For more than a hundred years, the Gettysburg photographs have remained in a confused and neglected state. Their value as historical documents was realized well before the turn of the century, but their value as historical source materials was basically left untapped. A large number of the views were arbitrarily attributed to the famous Mathew Brady; captions and dates were vague and often incorrect; significant relationships between scenes went unnoticed; and although the views appeared time and time again in monumental works such as Miller's ten-volume *Photographic History of the Civil War*, for all practical purposes no one thought to question the credits or the captions, or otherwise thought to treat the Gettysburg photographs as a distinct series.

By identifying the confusion that has existed, and by substituting order for that confusion, I have attempted to demonstrate what can be done—and indeed, what must be done—with historical photographs if they are ever to be accurately employed by students of the past.

The value of the early photograph is manifold. It is a unique document rich in information. It provides a dimension to the study of history available nowhere else. Moments in time have been captured and preserved, and it is for us today to be aware of the fact that unless such images are gathered, researched, organized, and used to the fullest, we will be doing ourselves, as well as the photographers who recorded them, a great injustice. The loss, however, will mainly be ours.

NOTES

1.   For a biography of Alexander Gardner, *see* Josephine Cobb, "Alexander Gardner," *Image: Journal of Photography* VII (June 1958): 124–136. For a biography of T. H. O'Sullivan, *see* Beaumont and Nancy Newhall, *Timothy O'Sullivan, Photographer* (Rochester, N.Y.: George Eastman House, 1966). Additional material may be found in James D. Horan, *Timothy O'Sullivan: America's Forgotten Photographer* (New York: Bonanza Books, 1966). Horan's works, however, must be used with caution. His information is frequently incorrect or misleading. Little is known of James Gibson. A discussion of Gibson's business association with Mathew Brady may be found in Josephine Cobb, *Mathew B. Brady's Photographic Gallery in Washington*, reprinted from *The Columbia Historical Society Records* (n.p., 1955), pp. 29, 33–36.

2.   All original Gardner captions and credits used in this work are from Alexander Gardner, *Catalogue of Photographic Incidents of the War* (Washington, D.C.: H. Polkinhorn, 1863). A copy of this exceedingly rare catalogue may be found in the Prints and Photographs Division of the Library of Congress.

3.   Cobb, "Alexander Gardner," p. 133.

4.   *New York Times*, October 20, 1862; *Harper's Weekly* VI (October 18,

1862): 663–665. At the time of his Antietam series, Gardner was still associated with Mathew Brady. Though individually copyrighted by Gardner, the Antietam photographs initially bore the label of "Brady's Album Gallery" series and were credited to Brady in *Harper's*. Not until the spring of 1863 would a formal break between the two men occur, Gardner retaining all rights to the views recorded at Antietam.

5.   Dr. Oliver Wendell Holmes, "Doings of the Sunbeam," *Atlantic Monthly* XII (July 1863): 11–12.

6.   Additional information concerning the wet plate process and its application during the Civil War may be found in Robert Taft, *Photography and the American Scene* (New York: Macmillan Co., 1938), pp. 233–234. Taft's book, readily available today in a paperback edition (New York: Dover Publications, 1964), is an indispensable source for any study concerning early American photography.

7.   Gardner would later assume credit for a number of the eight-by-ten-inch plates recorded at Gettysburg. According to the 1863 catalogue, however, the latter plates were all recorded by O'Sullivan. The eight-by-ten-inch plates were invariably duplicates of stereo subjects, taken from the identical camera position.

8.   Based on a comparative study of the following sources: Mrs. Tillie Alleman, *At Gettysburg: or What a Girl Saw and Heard of the Battle* (privately printed, 1888), p. 81; Frank A. Haskell, *The Battle of Gettysburg* (Madison, Wisconsin: Wisconsin History Commission, 1908), pp. 169–180; Daniel A. Skelly, *A Boy's Experiences during the Battles of Gettysburg* (Gettysburg, Pa.: D. A. Skelly, 1932), pp. 20–21; Lee, Nelson, Slack, *Revised Report of the Select Committee Relative to the Soldiers' National Cemetery* (Harrisburg, Pa.: Singerly and Myers, 1865), p. 150; Earl S. Miers, ed., *Gettysburg* (New Brunswick, N.J.: Rutgers University Press, 1948), p. 268; *New York Herald*, July 9, 1863; *New York Times*, July 9, 12, 1863; *Philadelphia Inquirer*, July 8, 11, 1863.

9.   For a well-documented account of Brady's career, see Cobb, *Mathew Brady's Photographic Gallery*. Further information may be found in James D. Horan, *Mathew Brady, Historian with a Camera* (New York: Crown Publishers, 1955). As with Horan's biography of T. H. O'Sullivan, this work must be used cautiously.

10.   *Harper's Weekly* VII (August 22, 1863): 529, 532–533.

NOTES

11. U.S. Surgeon General, *Medical and Surgical History of the War of the Rebellion*, Part II, Vol. II (Washington, D.C.: U.S. Government Printing Office, 1877), pp. 66, 92, 951. *See also* William H. Ridinger, "Hospitals at Gettysburg," (unpublished study, Gettysburg National Military Park, 1942), p. 54.

12. *Under the Maltese Cross, Antietam to Appomattox, Campaigns of the 155th Pennsylvania Volunteers* (Pittsburgh, Pa.: 155th Regimental Association, 1910), pp. 191–192.

13. Brady issued an incomplete catalogue of his Civil War scenes in 1869: *National Photographic Collection of War Views and Portraits of Representative Men* (New York: C. A. Alvord, 1869). Only seven of his Gettysburg views were listed in that publication.

14. Taft, p. 466, citing an article in the *Photographic Art Journal* I (1851): 138.

15. A biography of Charles J. Tyson may be found in M. A. Leeson, *History of Adams and Cumberland Counties* (Chicago: Warner Beers and Co., 1886), Part III, p. 478.

16. This story was told by Charles Tyson in a letter that appears in N. D. Preston, *History of the Tenth Regiment of Cavalry, New York State Volunteers* (New York: D. Appleton and Co., 1892), pp. 125–128. The original Tyson building is located one door east of Lincoln Square (the diamond), on the south side of York Street, Gettysburg.

17. *The Compiler* (Gettysburg), August 10, 1863.

18. *The Adams Sentinel* (Gettysburg), January 8, 1867.

19. This catalogue was examined and noted by Mr. William C. Darrah at the New York Public Library about 1948. Unfortunately, this most important document can no longer be located in the Library's collections.

20. Judging from the dilapidated condition of the Union breastworks in view III–4, together with the settled appearance of the Confederate grave in view III–12, it is suggested that the Weaver stereo series was recorded ca. 1864 rather than 1863. (*See* William C. Darrah, *Stereo Views, A History of Stereographs in America and Their Collection* [Gettysburg, Pa.: Times and News Publishing Co., 1964], p. 71.) Mr. Darrah's book contains a wealth of information on nineteenth-century photography and photographers.

21. Robert Fowler, "With Lincoln at Gettysburg," *Civil War Times Illus-*

trated II (November, 1963): 10, 21. The Weaver letter was uncovered by Miss Josephine Cobb.

22. Alexander Gardner, *Gardner's Photographic Sketch Book of the War* (Washington, D. C.: Philip and Solomons, 1866), caption for plate 41. The first book ever published to incorporate mounted photographs taken on Civil War battlefields, Gardner's work is today regarded as a classic. Of the one hundred prints included in this work, ten were recorded at Gettysburg. All of these were selected from the series of eight-by-ten-inch plates. While original editions of the *Sketch Book* are quite rare, an inexpensive reprint is currently available in paperback (New York: Dover Publications, 1959).

23. *New York Tribune,* July 11, 1863.

24. More on Tipton may be found in Leeson, p. 374. An autobiographical sketch written by Tipton in 1922 may be found at the National Park Service Visitor Center, Gettysburg. The Park Service also maintains a complete set of photographs printed from the Tipton negative collection.

25. Thomas Chamberlin, *History of the 150th Pennsylvania Volunteers* (Philadelphia: F. McManus, Jr., and Co., 1905), pp. 129–130. A second Bucktail regiment, the 143rd Pa., claimed that it was their color bearer, Sergeant B. Crippen, to whom General Hill was referring. The dispute was never settled.

26. Oddly enough, this tree does not show up in the companion stereo half. But because the center soldier's face is partially obliterated by negative damage in the scene reproduced here, it is the companion view that has often been published in prior works.

27. The Elliott map, undated but probably compiled in 1863. A copy may be found at the National Park Service Visitor Center, Gettysburg.

28. The story of Colonel Wheelock is fairly well-known. That of Private Hardman, however, is not. *See* Asa S. Hardman, "As a Union Prisoner Saw the Battle of Gettysburg," *Civil War Times Illustrated* I (July 1962): 46–50.

29. Robert L. Bloom, "Gettysburg College during the Civil War," *Gettysburg College Bulletin* LIII (July 1963): 9.

30. Ridinger, pp. 84–85.

31. Rev. W. R. Kiefer, *History of the 153rd Regt. Pennsylvania Vol. Infantry* (Easton, Pa.: Chemical Publishing Co., 1909), p. 219.

32.   Skelly, pp. 16–17.

33.   *Under the Maltese Cross*, p. 192.

34.   Francis T. Miller, ed., *The Photographic History of the Civil War* (New York: Review of Reviews Co., 1911), II, p. 263. This discovery was made by the author in January 1967. The same discovery, however, was made independently by a Mr. Fred Mende, whose information was the basis of an article entitled "Mystery of Gettysburg Photograph Solved," *Civil War Times Illustrated* IX (January 1971): 40–41.

35.   Fowler, p. 12.

36.   *Harper's Weekly* IX (July 22, 1865): 452–453.

37.   The Elliott map.

38.   Skelly, p. 20.

39.   One of the ten Gettysburg plates reproduced in Gardner's *Sketch Book* was a view of Meade's headquarters recorded during some later trip to the battlefield. That the view was not taken in July 1863 is clearly reflected by the barren trees. While it would be easy to consider this photograph as evidence supporting Gardner's claim to have attended the November 1863 dedication ceremonies, Gardner credits the negative to O'Sullivan, who was working in Virginia during the month of November 1863 (*Sketch Book*, plates 47, 48).

40.   The earliest known photographs taken specifically of the scene of Pickett's charge were recorded by William Tipton in 1881. They were commissioned by Paul Philippoteaux who used them as the basis for his painting of the charge. Copies of these photographs may be examined at the National Park Service Visitor Center, Gettysburg.

41.   Supported by a comparative study of contemporary accounts. See footnote 8.

42.   To the author's knowledge, the first person to become aware of the fact that the body was moved to the stone wall from some other location was Mr. Frederic Ray, art director of *Civil War Times Illustrated* (Frederic Ray, "The Case of the Rearranged Corpse," *Civil War Times* III [October 1961]: 19).

43.   Brooke's most advanced position, as indicated by his regimental monuments, was located just inside the original woodline.

44.   John P. Nicholson, ed., *Pennsylvania at Gettysburg* (Harrisburg, Pa.:

E. K. Meyers, 1893), I, pp. 70, 208, 263.

45. Dr. J. W. C. O'Neal. The manuscript records are maintained at the National Park Service Visitor Center, Gettysburg.

LIST OF PHOTOGRAPHS BY PHOTOGRAPHER

LIST OF PHOTOGRAPHS BY PHOTOGRAPHER

GETTYSBURG: A JOURNEY IN TIME

INDEX

GETTYSBURG: A JOURNEY IN TIME